Fluid Copyright © 2025 Susan Goodson.

This book may not be reproduced in any form except in the case of brief quotations embodied in articles or reviews without the express written permission from the author or Putnam & Smith Publishing Company.

Fluid is registered trademark of Susan Goodson and Putnam & Smith Publishing Company, Encino, California.

Fluid
by
Susan Goodson

Copyright © 2025

Putnam & Smith Publishing Company

Cover Design by: Brian Harris

Distributed by:
Putnam & Smith Publishing Company
15915 Ventura Boulevard, Suite 101
Encino, California 91436

www.putnamandsmithpublishing.com

Library of Congress Control Number: 2024944813

ISBN: 978-1-939986-51-1
Printed in the USA

DEDICATION

To all women…
Who have carried the world on their shoulders.
Who have felt lost and weary in their quest of knowing
who they are and what God's will is for them.
Who have wanted to give up but have chosen not to.
Who cried out and thought no one was listening.
I hear you.
I see you.
I honor your courage and brave spirit.
And so does GOD.
Let's gather at the table and share our hearts as
God takes us on a journey of faith and healing.

ACKNOWLEDGMENTS

It is with deep gratitude that I acknowledge these beautiful souls who have been a valuable part of the process in creating this book.

Marlene Murray for taking me to lunch and telling me this six-month program was meant to be a book, so write it.

Maureen Zimmer for being my first coaching client and who breathed belief into me that there was so much more for me to do.

Kimberly Hatcher who was a constant reminder that I could do this and never wavered in her support of who I was and where I was going.

Shauna Zimmer who worked diligently beside me in more ways than I can count. She helped me to slow down when I was running ahead of God. She helped me to trust the process and not give up. She worked tirelessly looking over content, making suggestions and took the attached workbook to another level by researching and adding scripture verses to keep me and those who are reading this book on track.

These amazing women who agreed to be the first to experience the Fluid six-month program and allowing me time to write the book as they read chapter after chapter and going deeper into the questions supplied in the workbook. Maureen, Terry, Lucia, Patty, and Shauna. I couldn't have done it without you.

My husband, children, grandchildren and numerous friends for always supporting my deep desires to make a difference in the world through my words and life experiences.

And to my dear friend, Brian Harris, who took my vision, gave his heart and soul to designing my logo, creating the book cover and workbook cover and for never tiring of my many questions and requests for changes. Contact Brian at behstudio@hotmail.com.

We are a village.

FLUID

PROLOGUE

I believe God opens doors in His perfect timing and when we're ready we see them open. At this point we are given an opportunity to either walk through them in faith or wait until another time.

We always have a choice.

Here's the story of how this became an idea for a book.

I have written three books and self-published each one. One was written about raising addict children while being an off and on-again single mom and a self-employed businesswoman in our community. The second one was about the lessons I've learned while in my quiet moments with God. The third and most recent one was on the conversations I have been having when I go to the riverbank in my mind to seek His wisdom, counsel and answers to my ongoing confusion, hunger for truth and His encouragement to always be brave and trust in Him.

After finishing my training to be a certified life, health, mastery, and transformational coach focusing on helping women gain clarity and how to live a more authentic and vibrant life I started seeking more answers in the direction I was heading.

I found myself continuing to do ongoing training by working with trained coaches on how to build a stronger and more lucrative business. It was quite costly, but I believed this was my next step.

After a year of continued education and working with some very special clients who had trusted me to be their guide as their life coach, the word "fluid" kept coming up in many of our conversations. I saw the word in magazines, on TV commercials and in my own life as I considered what living a life of freedom looked like.

FLUID was my word and now it was my intention, but what did that mean?

As I continued to listen over time, which felt like forever because if it isn't happening NOW it will never happen, the acronym became clear.

F - freedom

L - learning

U - understanding

I - intuition

D - dreaming

+ putting it all together to create the life you have longed to live.

Where was this going to take me? I wondered.

How did this divine download need to be implemented?

Who was it for?

And slowly the plan took on a life of its own. Or so I thought.

It was the design for a 6-month private coaching program I was to use in my practice.

The idea had come quickly but now it was time to create what the acronym was going to look like, and I was eager to begin.

I got the basics all figured out and decided to ask my Bible study leader, Marlene, what she thought about my program. I emailed it to her to see if she knew anyone she thought might benefit from a program like this.

She suggested we meet for lunch. So, the following Friday I met her at the local Applebee's.

I was feeling a bit anxious because when I share anything that comes from my heart, I risk criticism or an unenthusiastic response, I asked her what she thought

She LOVED the idea and said, "This is your next book."

Looking somewhat confused she smiled and continued.

"Susan, this program is amazing and so many women can be helped by what you're writing and how you're presenting it. The book is already here. You just need to add more details. And you could create a workbook to go along with it making room to answer questions, journal thoughts and get in touch with what the reader is feeling.

I would definitely introduce it to our pastor after it's completed and maybe it can be used as a resource for women to use together to go deeper into their own personal healing.

WOW was all I could think. Maybe this really is a possibility, but it seemed so big that I walked away with a sense of wonder and confusion trying to take in everything she said.

I drove home and instantly thought of my friend Shauna who has a beautiful and trusting relationship with the Lord. I called her to tell her what just happened. She giggled and told me she had the same thought the night before as she drifted off to sleep. Shauna had already known about the 6-month program I was putting together and was one of the first to say she'd jump in and be a part of its development.

We both agreed this was the confirmation needed to proceed but what next? I asked her if she'd be willing to help me create the workbook and add scripture verses to reinforce the Biblical truth that supported what God was having me write. She was thrilled and then reminded me that a year and a half earlier when we had begun our journey together as coach and client, we said we would one day work together. We laughed at the idea and moved on until the Friday I had lunch with my Bible study leader. The seed had been planted to go out on a limb with God and watch Him work.

It was then I realized the notion of truly stepping into the flow of His will as exhilarating, terrifying, and joyful all at the same time.

I was all in and scared to death.

And so, the beginning of birthing a book and workbook to help women dig deeper together for healing through community began.

FLUID:

FREEDOM from:

1. Others' opinions
2. Messages from the past
3. Old behaviors
4. Old thought patterns
5. My own judgement
6. Perfectionism
7. Overachieving
8. Fear
9. Procrastinating
10. Scarcity Mindset

LEARNING to:

1. Recognize my triggers.
2. How to stop "shoulding" (I should do….) on myself and others.
3. Stay in my own hula hoop.
4. Set stronger boundaries.
5. Let go of the voices of judgment I carry with me each day.
6. Replace fear with faith.
7. Letting a B- be good enough.
8. Accepting who I am, where I am, as I am.

UNDERSTANDING: who I am.

1. Childhood memories.
2. My own perfectly written novel. Looking at the chapters of my life and naming them.
3. What did I bring with me as truth from my childhood?
4. What ideas no longer feel in alignment with who I am and want to become?
5. Do I feel safe in my world today?

INTUITION: what's been calling me.

1. Are you an over thinker or over feeler?
2. Do you give yourself time each day to be still and listen to your intuitive voice?
3. What's your inner self calling you to do?
4. How do you feel when you hear that small little voice speaking?
5. When something doesn't feel right, do you feel it and honor it? If not, why?
6. Should I trust what I know?

DREAMING: can I really have what I want?

1. Where do I begin?
2. What do I WANT?
3. How do I give myself permission to dream again?
4. Am I willing to allow myself the time and space to start creating my own wish list?
5. When I think of my personal wants, what comes up for me?
6. Dream journal?
7. Finding my voice and asking for what I need and want.
8. Free to be me in all areas of my life.

Fluid…..

Oh, how I have longed to live a life that was more fluid.

- Not settled or stable; likely or able to change. "Our plans are still fluid."
- Smoothly elegant or graceful. "Her movements were fluid and beautiful to watch."
- To move with the flow of life without restriction, hesitation based on fear, or resistance due to stubbornness.

This word came to me early in 2022 as we were beginning to step back into life after Covid.

There was still some trepidation and fear and I found myself starting and stopping as I tried to live a life like the one I had lived prior to our two-year seclusion.

I soon understood that we were never going back to before and it was up to me to create a new normal for myself.

In those days following the lifted mask updates, I had an internal longing for something to settle my soul.

But what was that something?

Guaranteed safety no matter what I did or where I went?

Immediate success as I tried new avenues of work?

Smooth reentry into a world I was no longer sure about?

Lots of questions and no answers.

There was so much external noise vying for my ongoing attention that I couldn't hear myself think.

I chose to pause. Breathe. Listen.

Slowly the answers began to arrive with a beautiful feeling of infused light and a promise of more ease, balance, and grace.

As I continued to practice this new behavior of quiet trust, the word fluid continued to dance in my heart and reinforce I was headed in the right direction.

The way I wanted to breathe, to discover, to wander the slow lane for just a little while; to live, see and hear what was missing from my life.

ME!

I had mastered the art of doing and was yearning for more of the art of being.

I knew there had to be a change to create the life I wanted, but where did I start?

It had to start with me. I had resisted long enough. I couldn't keep telling God I wasn't capable because I knew HE was. Although my ego screamed for promises, an understanding of where this would go, would it be well received and a guarantee of great success, all I knew was He told me to write it. Let go, do what I was told and leave the rest to Him.

I had to surrender and begin with my willingness to listen to that small voice of the Holy Spirit prompting me with the next step.

The whisper said, "Go,"

And I did.

FLUID

CHAPTER 1

Freedom: *living without the influence from:*

1. Old behaviors
2. Messages from the past
3. Old behaviors
4. Old thought patterns
5. My own judgment
6. Perfectionism
7. Overachieving
8. Fear
9. Procrastinating
10. Scarcity mind set

One - Old behaviors:

Have you promised yourself you are not going to say certain words or not behave in certain ways only to find yourself doing exactly what you swore you wouldn't do?

Me too.

Why can't I do it better?

What's wrong with me that I keep doing what I say I won't?

There's nothing wrong.

It's human nature.

Old behaviors tend to live in our cells. In our DNA. They are automatic.

They are our auto response behaviors.

When we are triggered, we do what we've always done.

We reach for the only ways we know, even when they're not the choices we want to make.

Quite often we react with old patterns when we're angry, hungry, lonely, or tired.

How many times have you been on the run all day, exhausted from the many things calling for your attention and you're starving?

Instead of going home and making a healthy salad you just do what's easy and quick.

You do what you always do.

You run through the drive thru and you get your steady and reliable comfort food.

You deserve it.

It's been a long day and who has time to go home and cook or prepare a healthy meal?

And then later, maybe that night or early the next morning, you promise yourself, yet again, to do it differently the next time.

Behavior change is not easy. It requires concentrated effort, and it takes time.

So, when you're sick and tired of being sick and tired you will slow down long enough to invite new possibilities into your mind.

You can choose to set aside a couple hours each weekend to plan your meals for the week and do some meal prep.

You can make a list of healthy foods you want to add into your daily food routine.

You can take charge of your mental and physical health and stop blaming your behaviors on current situations in your life.

It's YOUR life.

You can make the changes if you want new results.

Is it easy? Heck no.

It's challenging, frustrating, exhausting, and painful. For a while.

But if you stop and really look at where you are now, doing what you're doing, aren't the end results challenging you, frustrating you, causing you to be mentally and physically fatigued, overwhelmed and in pain?

Well, if that's how you're going to feel either way, wouldn't you feel more accomplished and fulfilled with the effort to bring about new and healthier results?

How can you know unless you try?

When you make the healthier choice, give yourself a high five for your willingness to step into a new place of change.

And when you choose to do what you've done before, which you will do, give yourself some grace and remember that there are no right or wrong decisions. There are simply choices that will bring about different consequences.

You are not perfect.

You weren't meant to be.

One day, one choice at a time. And this has to do with all our old ways of doing things.

Getting angry at our children or spouses when things we've planned go awry.

Becoming aggressive with fellow employees when someone promises to do something, and they don't follow through.

Becoming distant and refusing to discuss certain situations because we are struggling with resentment, and we don't want to be honest about how we feel.

By the way, when it comes to any choice we are faced with, I'd like to suggest these simple steps.

When you're reaching for anything that brings you comfort, be it TV binging, food filled with sugar, caffeine or excess carbohydrates, alcohol, cigarettes, or drugs, pause for a moment and take a deep breath. Hold your hands up, palms facing outwards and say out loud, "STOP." Break the thought cycle long enough to check in with yourself and ask, "What kind of comfort am I hungry for right now?"

1. Are you exhausted and what you need is rest?
2. Could you possibly be dehydrated and need a tall glass of cool refreshing water?
3. How long has it been since you had something to eat? Maybe you're simply hungry for some healthy food.
4. Are you angry and you'd rather stuff yourself with food than talk about it?
5. You're lonely, missing a loved one, so disconnected from yourself that you miss YOU and need some time with a friend? Need a hug?
6. Or could it be you're longing for some quiet and intimate time with God?

No matter what the reason might be, if you can pause before you reach for that remote control, sugar, caffeine or carbohydrates, extra glass of red wine, a Zanax or a Marlboro (whatever you use to numb the pain) and consider what you really need deep down inside, you can choose with a clear head and be more proactive rather than reactive.

Even if you decide the comfort fix is what you want at least you can own it and not regret it later.

Every day can bring opportunities of awareness and with those ah ha moments we stand in a place where we can make different choices.

It happened for me one day on a coaching call with a client who had signed up to be in my first 6-month fluid program. We had known each other for about 10 years, and she was ready now to step into a bit more coaching, seeking deeper transformational change.

Her circumstances with her husband are like mine, and we talked many times on my front porch while sharing an iced vanilla coffee.

On this call, she became the teacher and I, the student.

I was in awe at the realizations she was having and felt conflicted with each thought she shared.

It had to do with owning her choices and no longer being willing to be a victim of her life as it was today.

What can you do to remind yourself to pause before you act?

How can you quiet your mind long enough to reason out what your next step is?

And what words can you speak to your inner child to help them relax and be more open to the changes that are coming?

How can you support yourself in this journey in the best possible ways?

This journey doesn't happen overnight. It takes time to unlearn what we have known our whole life and replace toxic behaviors with newer, healthy ones. It starts with an awareness of what we do that no longer serves us. Then we get the chance to seek out what might be new ways we want to live. We get to try something different for a while.

If it doesn't feel right, we get to set it aside. And try again.

I know you have heard the quip "When God closes a door, He always opens a window."

But I heard an extension to that which said, When God closes a door, He always opens a window. But it sure is hell in the hallway."

When we understand what we don't want to do anymore, we are often not clear on what we need to do to replace what we're letting go of. It's ok to sit in that space of uncertainty and allow our spirit to go quiet until the answers come because they will.

✎ Grab your workbook and start journaling.

Two - Messages from the past/present.

What are those messages that still haunt us from our childhood?

Why can't you be more like your sister/brother?

What's wrong with you?

If you keep eating sugar, you'll get fat, and who will ever want to be your friend?

If you speak too loud or act too strongly, who will want to marry you?

You're just too much. Too smart, too creative, too strong, too independent.

TOO. TOO.TOO.

Don't speak up. No one wants to hear what you have to say.

You talk too much.

Why can't you listen more?

You're not trying hard enough.

I can still hear the whisper of those words sometimes, but decided to take this to God and share how I was feeling.

At the riverbank....

I walked a bit slowly today as I was exhausted from living in over 100-degree heat for the last couple weeks.

God greeted me with an iced cold lemonade and a smile.

"How did you know I needed this right now?"

He laughed. "You really need to ask that? I know EVERYTHING, especially when my children are weary and thirsty."

I smiled.

God continued, "Anything on your mind?"

"There's always something on my mind." I replied.

"So what's up?" He asked.

"Well, it has to do with knowing what Your will is and how to be sure I'm doing what you're calling me to do. I get so confused sometimes and find myself stuck in my need to know exactly what I'm supposed to do next."

"Sounds pretty complicated to Me," He said.

"Child, My will isn't meant to be complicated and confusing. That's what happens when you get caught up in overthinking and then letting your need to do everything right stop you. These are old ways you have learned from childhood. Not everything you've learned is true today.

You were raised by parents who had their own wounds and filters and a society that has created its own rules. You must use discernment when it comes to making choices and decisions."

"How can I do that Lord? I want to do the right thing." I said.

"Do you believe there can be more than one right thing you can do?"

"Hmm. I never really thought there could be more than one way to do Your will. I am always trying to find that one thing and doing it perfectly."

He laughed. "Honey, there is no perfect way. Who told you you had to be perfect? That wasn't Me. That message came from somewhere else. It's a lie.

All I want is for you to be still and listen.

Ask Me what you need to know, be quiet and just do the next thing. If it's making breakfast, make breakfast. If it's taking the kids to school, then take the kids to school. Going to work, get to work.

My will is meant to be simple. But it does require trust, courage, and action."

"It sounds so easy." I replied.

"It's simple, but not easy. It requires you to pause and recognize when your actions are being prompted by unhealthy motives. And humans don't like to slow down. They often function on auto pilot."

"Boy, do I get that."

"I know you do. Slowing down is not easy for you. My heart overflows when I watch you seek to do what I'm asking especially when it's such a struggle. Your act of simply trying to do better each day brings Me joy."

"How do I let go of old behaviors and thoughts? I asked.

"Seek the truth in My Word. Talk with others who know and love Me. Pause, breathe and check in with how you will feel if you say what you're about say and do what you're about to do.

If you are in touch with Me, you will know."

I looked down and found my hand in His and said, "Thank You for always holding on to me."

"You can count on it."

I am learning to recognize the voices of my saboteurs who want to recycle old messages to keep me in check. They are voices of my family, teachers, neighbors, and any others who I trusted to be truth tellers.

I now know they were simply sharing the messages they received as they grew up.

What they learned, they taught me. And they were doing the best they could through their own filter of what was true then.

As I continue my growth process, I am reminded that there may be feelings that arise around shedding those old messages. If I let go of what I was taught, am I betraying or disrespecting my parents? Do I need to keep believing their beliefs or can I give myself permission to let those go? Am I turning my back on them if I choose to release what they passed down from generations before them? I had to really pray about that, as I didn't want to continue to let myself down to keep others happy, even my mom and dad.

But then again didn't they teach me to be an independent thinker? Hmm. Not really. My dad had his own issues of control and my mom lived in constant fear, so when I honestly look at my background I can say I was more influenced not to question authority or rock the boat than speak up and seek more clarity and understanding.

It wasn't until many years later I began to sense a shift inside and a new consciousness coming alive as to whether what they held as truth still resonated with me as mine. The answer was no.

I had to make the tough decision to disappoint them rather than continue to betray myself.

I was afraid I would be abandoned for standing up for myself. But it was paramount that I find the courage to stop bowing down to those who loved me but whose influence was no longer healthy or applicable.

To my amazement they accepted my choices and honored who I was.

Can you relate?

It is vital you be willing to do what God is asking you to in this season, even if it makes you feel vulnerable. It's through this that you will learn to trust Him more, grow your faith, and begin to understand who He created YOU to be.

✎ Please go to your workbook and take some time to write out your thoughts and answers.

Three - Other's opinions - What will the neighbors think?

How many times have you been stopped in your tracks thinking about what the neighbors would think? You know those old voices ingrained from childhood still living in your subconscious after how many years?

Too many.

But how can we change that and let go of beliefs we were taught and have been inundated with since childhood?

It requires thoughtful time away from the noise of the world so you can listen to what your own internal voice is saying.

As far as the belief of what will the neighbors think I'll bet that was the voice of your parents and not your voice. It was their insecurity of how your behaviors would reflect on them as parents. It was their egos wanting to protect themselves from what THEIR neighbors would say.

We were kids. I'm not sure we gave much thought as to what the world was thinking until we learned from others it was important. It never really crossed my mind of what others might be thinking because I was busy trying to live/survive my childhood.

There were secrets in our home, but I never thought of telling anyone because the culture I lived in was one of secrecy.

As I look back, I can see now it was the secrets of my parents that caused them fear and trepidation of being exposed.

It wasn't until I became a parent that I even began to consider the notion of what others might think of what was going on in my home. As a child I never gave much thought to it.

Today, after raising three children who struggled with addiction, I can say, having done my own deep dive work around my childhood messages, I can recognize that the behaviors of my children belong to them. But it doesn't always hold as true when I am in times of physical and emotional exhaustion. It is in those times I forget what I know and wander into the space of how people will judge me if my kids are not performing to their greatest potential.

I can clearly remember those moments when I was horrified to think that my Mary Kay clients might hear about how one of my kids was going to jail for something I had no clue was going on? Did I have trouble believing if they knew what was happening behind closed doors, they would dump me as their beauty consultant because they judged me as an irresponsible mother?

Of course, I had those moments.

I am human and even with the emotional work I had done I was never fully rid of the embarrassment I held when I thought my personal life would be found out and I would be labeled as a fraud. It has taken many years to learn to let go of the idea that I'm not responsible for anyone's behavior other than mine.

I heard someone share the idea that my children's problems may have my name on them, but the solutions have their name on them. What that means is I may have been the source of their problems because of my own dysfunctional behavior but how they heal and the solutions they need must be their responsibility. For example, my dad being an angry alcoholic caused me many problems growing up, even into my adulthood. But I am the only one who can seek healing and resolution for this.

There were too many times to count when I had to pause, take a deep breath and remind myself I didn't teach these children to drink, smoke, steal, cheat or the many other things addicts do when they are under the influence.

And for those who passed judgment on me as their mother for behaviors they were choosing I had to let go of what they thought as they were not living in my shoes or living my life.

It's okay to release old beliefs and allow yourself to choose what you believe and live your truth honestly and authentically.

Giving credibility to what others think also means we give our power away. We can no longer trust what we know instinctively to be true for ourselves. When we try go into the heads of anyone other than us, we are creating thoughts they might not even be thinking. We are thinking

FLUID

FOR them and then living what we think is in their minds as our truth.

There is a saying that is: "You wouldn't know worry about what others are thinking of you if you realized they rarely thought of you at all".

✎ Grab your workbook, turn to the questions for this chapter and write your thoughts before you forget them. I promise you if you think you will come back later you may not remember what your heart was feeling right now.

Four - Old thought patterns

Our old way of thinking is often what causes us to continue to do the things we no longer want to do. We think it and then we act on it.

Where do they come from? I think we know many of these patterns were created in childhood as ways of coping in our lives and trying to find meaning to what was going on outside of ourselves.

These are the voices of our saboteurs, and it is said we have nine saboteurs.

(FOOTNOTE: I was taught this through a yearlong mental fitness study taught by Shirzad Chamine at Positive Intelligence. If you'd like more information or would like to take the assessment test to see what your top 3 saboteurs are, visit www.positiveintelligence.com or reach out to me and I can help you with that. I offer a free 6-week course with my six-month private coaching program or you can contact me at sgoodsonmk@gmail.com)

We all have the voice of the judge.

The whisper that says you're not enough.

They're not enough.

And nothing is enough.

It constantly reminds us of our past mistakes, failures, and why nothing is ever going to be good enough unless we are perfect and work harder. Those messages are lies and until we can learn to stop believing them, we will live in our pain and struggle throughout our lifetime.

I have experienced a life of anxiety and worry and couldn't seem to stop the cycle of thoughts that fed my fears. It was nonstop. No matter how hard I prayed, surrendered, let go and journaled, they just kept showing up.

When healthy thoughts become toxic, life gets toxic.

My relationships start to deteriorate.

I can only see the bad in others because that's all I can see in myself.

The judgmental voice gets louder.

My thoughts lose clarity and I get stuck in a pattern I can't escape from.

After I did my own assessment test, I had a better understanding of what was happening and how to change those cycles of destructive thought patterns.

Along with the Judge these two saboteurs, the Pleaser and the Hyper Vigilant, were strong influences on my behavior.

The Pleaser is the voice that tells me I need to make everyone happy, satisfy everyone's needs, help with the world's problems, and fix every hurt. Not doing so will leave me abandoned and rejected.

It takes my gifts of generosity, kindness and wanting good for others to the extreme. Then my deep desire to be accepted and loved ends up overshadowing my own personal needs. I lose myself in the wants of others and find myself resentful and quietly angry all the time.

Currently I am working on honoring my yeses and nos. What I mean is when asked to do something (before I put my hand up and jump in full force), I take 24 hours to pray about it and if necessary, seek counsel from others. I stop and pause so I can check in with what my motives are for wanting to help. Is it because I want to be the hero again and save the world? If so, that's my ego prompting me. Do I fear what you will think of me if I decline to help? That's my people pleaser nature wanting to take over. Do I think you cannot do what you're asking help for on your own and I must step in to make life easier for you? That's my pride.

I used to think that helping was one of my greatest gifts and, when done from a place of healthy respect for myself and others, it is. But if I am doing for you what you are clearly capable of doing yourself, I have crossed a line and stepped in where God hasn't called me to be.

How many times have I said yes when I wanted to say no because I thought you'd be angry if I didn't help you reach a goal that maybe God didn't want you to have from the beginning? I look back and can see how much my motivation was truly to please me rather than God and seek recognition that never belonged to me in the first place.

The hyper-vigilant voice is the one that tries to protect me from future crises that may be headed my way.

These three saboteurs stem from the fear of death that lived in my home growing up.

This will be discussed a bit more in the heading of fear but here is a short version of my childhood.

My dad was constantly sick and frequently hospitalized while my was mom was home, taking care of four children, while being afraid my dad would never make it home from the hospital.

Fear was palpable and I absorbed it.

From early in childhood, I have fought the voice that says something bad is going to happen. Stay awake. Watch out. Listen. Observe. Think. Stop. When's the next shoe going to drop?

This manifested in my hyper-vigilant behaviors around my health. When my outside circumstances became too much to deal with, I would start paying extra attention to my body. I would scan everything from head to toe and if one thing was not in perfect alignment, I ended up in a full-blown panic attack.

A headache meant a brain tumor.

An itch behind my ear became ringworm.

Growing pains in my legs became an autoimmune disease.

It was always something, and I could never rest because I was so focused on losing control. There wasn't anything outside me I could control, so instead I would hold on to my fear of the unknown. It's a wonder I never ended up with an eating disorder, which my mom did suspect after I was first married.

I drove my parents crazy with all the things that were going wrong with me.

But there was never anything wrong other than the coping mechanisms

I created to keep me safe. Could this have been my rebellion to all the attention going to my dad and the rest of my family because of their health issues? Was I afraid of going invisible in my own family if something wasn't terribly wrong with me? How could I fit in this family if I wasn't sick too and needing medical attention?

One of my brothers stuttered when he was young and needed to see a speech therapist.

My sister had asthma and had to be hospitalized.

My next brother was found blue in his crib when he was a few days old and was diagnosed with a heart condition, and the youngest ended up needing a kidney transplant as an adult.

These thoughts were exhausting, and I was tired of thinking.

Even up to a year or so ago I was interpreting my physical symptoms as a possible heart problem or effects of high blood pressure, which only added more stress to my current situation of being a caregiver.

Worry was making the symptoms worse.

It was then I discovered the work of Shirzad and chose to step into his teaching on how to be mentally fit and use the techniques to build new neural pathways in my brain. I wanted to stop the destructive patterns of pessimism, both physical and mental, that I so wanted to be rid of.

Since then, I have continued to study his teachings and have found myself more peaceful, my spirit calmer, the voice of reason and truth surfacing more often and the cries of fear and distress diminishing.

Does that voice still come up and haunt me? Absolutely.

A couple of weeks ago when we went with my son and fiancé to pick up our granddaughters at the airport, I recognized I had an ache in my right calf. Although I didn't want to jump to serious conclusions, I did call my daughter who is a nurse and asked her what she thought. Katie asked the appropriate questions: Swelling in my leg? No. Red? Hot to the touch? No. Any history of our family having blood clots? No.

I decided there was nothing wrong and went about my daily business.

But there was that little small voice inside whispering that it wasn't totally sold on the idea it was a strained calf muscle. Instead of the usual panic I stopped, paused, and took the next indicated step.

Thursday, I emailed my doctor to tell her what was going on. She sent back a message at 5:03 p.m. suggesting I get a blood test.

A blood test? What in heaven's name for? I didn't really have any symptoms to speak of. I decided to wait and get the test done the following week since I was planning on going to the beach with my husband on Friday, Knott's Berry Farm with family Saturday, getting our teeth cleaned on Monday and attending a stepdaughter's wedding in La Jolla on Wednesday and Thursday.

However, there were different plans at work I was not aware of.

An hour and a half into our beach trip my husband got sick, and he wanted to go home. The drive, with traffic, was almost two hours. We canceled our dinner plans with a friend and took off for Riverside as quickly as I could pack up the car.

I had a hunch that I could make it to the lab at Loma Linda before they closed so I asked my husband if he could tolerate an extra twenty minutes so I could run and get the lab work done.

He said he was good enough to do that, so instead of home we went straight to Loma Linda.

It was 2:30 p.m. by the time we arrived and 3:00 p.m. when we finally left to hit the freeway home.

At 5:03 p.m. I got an email that said my numbers were high and my doctor was ordering a stat ultrasound of the leg at a local imaging clinic. The only problem was the clinic was closed until Monday.

I paused, took a breath, got home, and called a friend who is a nurse practitioner.

After our call, the decision was made to go back to Loma Linda's 24-hour urgent care. I called a friend to go with me and within roughly two hours an ultrasound revealed a substantial clot behind my knee.

FLUID

After more blood tests I was admitted to the hospital at 3:00 a.m. prescribed blood thinners and release at 2:30 p.m. the following day.

I have not been in the hospital since my knee replacement five years ago and this time everything was so different.

I wasn't filled with the usual anxiety, especially when my friend had to leave me there at 11:30 p.m. to go home.

I used the calming techniques I learned through positive intelligence and my blood pressure remained normal even though I am on blood pressure meds.

There was virtually no apprehension, and my spirit was peaceful throughout the ordeal.

I was able to recognize the voice of fear when it tried to rear its ugly head and I spoke out loud calling it a liar.

I then simply implemented the technique called P.Q's which is rubbing my index finger against my thumb with enough tension to feel the ridges on my fingers tips for at least 20 seconds and the slow, boiling, panic that wanted to creep into the dark night diminished and I was again at peace.

The techniques are so simple, and I can't wait to share them with you as we continue our journey together.

There are many subtle ways we use to cope when life gets scary. It's the thoughts we think that create the behaviors we use to momentarily ease the pain that might be coming up.

Maybe its food. We eat to stuff our feelings, our confusion, our lack of trust in the world, our anger, anxiety, and terror.

Or it could be sugar. Exercise. Self-negligence around our own care. Alcohol, drugs, and work. When the motive is to stop pain, it can become a problem.

I'd like you to try something for me.

Stop and take a deep breath. Close your eyes.

Now take your index finger and your thumb and rub them together with enough tension to feel the ridges of the skin on your fingertips. Do this for about 20 seconds while being mindful of your breathing.

This simple technique can stop the cycle of thinking that keeps looping in your brain creating confusion and panic. This gives your body and mind a chance to be still for a moment and regroup. This practice creates new neuro pathways and shifts your brain so slowly you can begin to live in a place of a healthier mindset. I know this idea may not be clear. All I am asking you to do is the exercise and see what happens in the moment. Take time to journal.

✎ Turn to the workbook and answer this question. How did this exercise help me?

Five - My own judgment:

We talked a bit about this in the previous chapter.

The way we use our thought to judge what we have done or haven't done.

The things we could have done better.

The way we "should" on ourselves.

It's what we think that keeps us in check and makes us strive harder to achieve greatness.

This is the lie I have told myself for a long time, that I needed the judge to make me accountable. To make me stronger. To keep me focused. To make me learn a lesson.

The judge is the voice that pours shame and guilt all over us with each step we take.

You could have, should have blah, blah, blah.

NO. That's not the most helpful way to go about it.

It not only criticizes me but everyone and everything around me. It's not the voice of God. It's the voice of a sick society, wounded parents, and unhealthy friends. If it can convince me to hold myself to unattainable standards, then it can create a mindset of impossibility and unrealistic goals that I can then transfer to you. It's the voice of continual set up for failure.

It is so subtle that often I don't recognize it speaking because it's so familiar.

Only when I can slow down in my daily living and get quiet for a few minutes to check in with where I am, what I'm doing and how I'm feeling can I detect it and make the necessary changes to plug into God's voice.

What we need is the voice of wisdom drawing us into our greatest calling.

Take a minute to remember back to the times when, at the end of a workday, your boss came at you with all the tasks needed to be done before heading home from work and exactly how it should be done.

Did you enthusiastically run forward with joy in your heart to get those chores done?

I certainly didn't.

My spirit instantly became resistant, and my invisible walls went up while secretly saying to myself I don't think so. You're not the boss of me. Well maybe you are the boss of me but I'm still not going to do it and if I do, I am going to be angry the whole time.

So even if it was a good thing for me to do, I was not going to do it.

But what if that same person came to me and said, "I can see you're tired and today has been a long day. Before we leave, I need a bit of help. Could you assist me in getting _____ done so we can complete it more quickly together?

The result would have been the same. The job would be finished but the way the need was communicated brought me forward into the situation with kindness rather than force.

It makes all the difference.

Today when the voice of judgment is pushing me to do something with criticism and force, I can simply say out loud, "STOP." I hear you. Thank you for trying to keep me in check and on the right path. However, I am no longer willing to be forced in an abusive and aggressive way to get something done.

Instead, I am going to congratulate myself on what I have accomplished up to this point, pause and take a breath and then move into what needs to be done with an attitude of kindness and appreciation for who I am and what I bring to this space and time of my day and life.

The voice of the judge told us we need this voice. It's what keeps us aware and on task. It helps us want to do better. It encourages us to get things done.

But the opposite is true. It hounds us. It creates a spirit of frustration, and it is a constant push to do better, be better, do more, get more, have more. It's the pushing that causes us to self-destruct.

When we are being guided into something we lean in with little or no resistance because we are curious. We want to be led. We trust more when we feel safe about what we are being guided into. We no longer need to fight against what we're being asked to do but rather filled up as we are encouraged to come along and be a part of something.

Pay attention to when you are most susceptible to this voice of criticism and judgment so you can be aware when the triggers come. When you hear that voice call out the judge, tell him you no longer need him to hold you accountable. You must no longer believe the lies he tells.

Instead, step away, close your eyes, catch your breath, and replace that voice with the soft messages from the one who loves you and accepts you right where you are.

✎ It's time to turn to your workbook and take a look at the questions that will help you go deeper.

Six - Perfectionism:

Whoever told us that being perfect was a way of life? A good standard we should strive for? The definition of success? Be perfect in everything you do or don't do it.

Who said we had to do everything right and who defined what was right in the first place?

Where does perfectionism come from and whose voice is it that's telling us how we should do anything?

As I grew up, I had many messages from my parents about " if you can't do it right the first time why do it at all".

What a dumb thought.

How can I learn anything if I'm not willing to try and fail? Who can be perfect at anything anyway, especially when we are learning a new skill or task?

I believe we strive to be perfect to gain the love, approval and attention of those we love and depend on. I desperately wanted to please my parents because I didn't want to be abandoned. I wanted to be good enough but when I started striving to be who they needed me to be instead of who I really was I ended up crossing my own line of integrity to ensure I would never lose them. The cost was high and as I grew into adulthood, I realized my need for approval had shifted from my mom and dad to other authority figures and the cycle continued.

It was my feeling of unworthiness that kept me in that place of always needing to be the best, getting it right all the time, never letting up on myself to accept myself right where I was.

I was so afraid I would disappear that I was willing to do anything to stay on top and in front of those I so desperately wanted to like me.

(The list below is part of the training from Shirzad Chamine and Positive intelligence.)

Some of the characteristics of a person who carries perfectionism traits are:

They are punctual and methodical.

They can be irritable, tense, opinionated and sarcastic.

Strong need for self-control.

Works overtime to make up for others' sloppiness and laziness.

Is highly sensitive to criticism.

The thoughts they carry are:

Right is right and wrong is wrong. I know the right way.

If you can't do it perfectly, don't do it at all.

I need to be more organized and methodical than others so things get done.

I hate mistakes.

The lies they believe are:

It's up to me to fix whatever mess I encounter.

Perfectionism is good. Plus, it makes me feel good about myself.

I know how things should be done and must do the right thing.

Remember we are not perfectionists. We are people who have perfectionistic character traits that have been learned along the way of our lives.

However, when we get caught in those behaviors we create environments which feed resentment, anxiety, self-doubt, and resignation. We feel constantly criticized and resign ourselves to the fact that no matter how hard we work, we will never please our boss or authority figure.

Doing a good job, your best on any given day, with the tools you have is enough. But society, your boss and family may not have the same thought. Perfectionism is a fear-based way of living. It is triggered by unrealistic expectations.

I remember when I worked for others and always gave more than my share, over 100%. I went in early and stayed late. I asked what else needed to be done and how I could help. I did the work of others who were unwilling to do their share. I gave until I had nothing left to give and resented those who did only what they needed to get by and appease the boss.

I watched my fellow workers get praise when their usual 50% efforts went to 75% and then I was criticized when my 150% slipped to only 100%. I was angry all the time.

It wasn't until my daughter began sharing the same story of how she felt taken advantage of and used by her bosses for having a work ethic that was stronger than others that I could see she was following my example of trying to be perfect and the hero for others.

We talked at length about where that example came from and how it was motivated not from feeling good about what we were doing but our need for acceptance and approval. I apologized for teaching her that and asked how I could help her replace those patterns with healthier behaviors.

She and I could learn together, and it would require courage to set some powerful boundaries. It had to do with learning to say no without offering explanations. It was about doing our part, no more and no less. It was about letting others reap the consequences of not doing what they were being paid to do. It was about letting go of control over others and just taking care of what I could.

If I were in a management position it would become clear that I was responsible to communicate what was necessary and needed to get the job done but not stand there and force them to do it. If they were unwilling to do their jobs, then what came next was on them and not me.

I had to grow my confidence knowing my value so that if my superiors told me I would be fired if I didn't continue giving more than I could then I would be okay finding a healthier place to work where I would be appreciated for my efforts and not scolded for not doing more.

It sounds so simple and as we grow it does become simpler but rarely is it easy. It does require us to trust our value, put our brave face in front of our fearful face and ask for what we need and want.

✏️ Open your workbook and begin discovering more about who you are through the questions.

Seven - Over-achieving

Who am I if I don't have that trophy? That title? That car or home or job or whatever?

How many titles, degrees or accolades do I require to fill that hole in my soul that says I am not enough?

I was an entrepreneur for 43 years. I was always in hustle mode, making it happen. Being on alert with what was necessary to reach the next goal and earn the next prize.

It was an exhausting journey and I bought into the lie that "if it is to be, it's up to me." I carried so much responsibility on my shoulders I could barely make it through a day where I wasn't emotionally spent and resentful at everyone around me for not doing their part.

I did it all, all the time. I worked hard and never allowed myself time to play.

Growing up with a workaholic dad modeled for me what success looked like. I thought making money and having "stuff" was the answer to me feeling whole and alive in my business.

I never gave up and kept setting bigger goals, being more diligent, staying focused and praying for greater results. My need to do more, get more, have more and be more only made the hole inside grow deeper and wider. Nothing was ever going to be enough until I was willing to let it all go and stand there in my shame and sadness and forgive myself for all the lies I had believed.

There is no shame in being me, but it took me a long time for that belief to travel from my head into my heart.

It wasn't until I retired that I could even recognize who I was, where I was and what I believed.

Was setting goals and achieving the next title a bad thing? Not necessarily. But if my motive behind those goals was to prove to others I had value in what I did instead of who I was, then it could become a problem.

As I moved through my office observing what hung on my walls and what those things were saying to me, I decided to remove all the plaques and throw them away. Many of the prizes I had earned I gave to those who could use them. I went through my closets and donated all my business suits to the Pink Ribbon thrift store for women recovering from cancer.

I didn't want to live in the accomplishments of the past but rather to be present in the moment.

I'm sure many of my friends would think this might be over the top or a bit drastic but I no longer needed to be reminded of what I had done. I knew what I had achieved, and I didn't want to live in the mindset of the hustle or the prizes to make me loveable or of value to the world. And I didn't need anyone to understand or give me permission to do what I knew was right for me.

I wanted to have a more fluid life where I could move in the flow of God's will with little to no resistance and embrace the joy of being messy in the process of growing.

Overachievers are dependent on constant performance for self-respect and self-validation. They are barely getting one goal finished before moving on to the next and the next and the next. They focus on external validation as well and the acceptance and attention of others.

This leads to unsustainable workaholic tendencies.

They are competitive, image and status conscious.

They are good at covering up insecurities and adapt their personality to fit what would be most impressive to others.

They work hard and are often financially secure but at the cost of their happiness. Nothing is ever enough, and they find themselves feeling empty no matter how much they have accomplished. There is never an end to the road of achievement, and nothing changes until they become acutely aware of what they are losing. For example: their families, their friendships, and their health.

Sometimes it takes a critical and dire diagnosis to stop an over achiever in their tracks and force them into reevaluating what's most important to them.

I'm grateful I could see that burnout had arrived and it was time for me to let go and retire from my position as a sales director. I hadn't been diagnosed with any illness, but I was having to give more attention to my husband whose health was starting to fail, and it was becoming clearer that the path I had been on needed to be changed and redirected.

I began studying to be a life coach a couple years prior and was working with a few select clients while taking care of a Mary Kay unit of 62-75 woman, over 100 clients and being the bread winner for our family.

I was headed for trouble and didn't even know it.

As I continued gathering more knowledge and tools to expand my coaching business and working with my own personal coach, the Lord brought to mind that I should rebrand myself as a "Intuitive Clarity Coach." I could come alongside women who were moving into a new phase of life and help them find clarity through clearing their physical and mental clutter. Along with letting go of excess, they could begin to hear the small voice of the Holy Spirit whispering to their intuition and gently guiding them to their next chapter of life. Along this path they would discover what their hearts were calling them to do and gain the confidence needed to make their course corrections.

It sounded perfect and I was thrilled. Until I got the message it was time to retire after 41 years in my leadership position. At which point my feathers rose up and I dug my feet firmly into the ground.

NOPE. I wasn't leaving Mary Kay. I could do both.

I had been divorced so I knew what new beginnings were all about. It was a no brainer. Coach and director. Simple. Right?

God's response was a bigger and stronger "NOPE!"

"That's not My plan. You cannot teach what you are not living."

I sat and stewed on what I knew was the right thing to do and then realized my unit was struggling to meet monthly production. Without my 25% we would slip below what was necessary and after two months the unit would fold and be taken in by another director.

Ok. I could do that.

His response, yet again was, "NOPE."

"Nope?" I asked.

"Nope. I am not going to let your people fail in order for you to not take responsibility for what I am asking you to do. Your team will continue to make production without you and will make money. I am not asking you to give me a dying business but a lucrative one and then pass your people on to the woman who has been your greatest competitor."

"What?" You must be joking Lord."

"Nope."

He likes that word. Or at least HE likes it with me.

I had a come to Jesus moment and it became so clear to me that I could choose to do what I wanted or to surrender completely to His lead and trust this new path.

It was so painful. I was scared. I was letting go of how I made money. My new business was not up and running yet and I couldn't see more than my next step which was often foggy. What I did see was that I trusted my ability to make money more than I trusted Him.

Ouch.

Let go was my daily message. Leave it all at My feet. I've got you. Wait. Surrender your dreams to Me.

I am in a perpetual state of learning. It's in surrender that we can make changes necessary to allow ourselves to reconcile that we are okay BEING rather than achieving.

My hope is that we can all begin to make changes before being forced with a life-or-death illness.

Generally, our patterns of behavior are created in our growing up years and they become our "go to" ways of doing things as survival skills. They served us when we were younger, but they cause chaos and disruption when we get older.

Think back to a time when you believed you were only valued when you were performing or accomplishing something.

Were you recognized by those you loved only when you were on the top of your game? Did you find yourself dependent on constant performance for your own sense of self respect? Was your need for external validation and acceptance at the forefront of your mind?

Were you thinking thoughts like "if I can't be outstanding, I won't bother." Or "I am worthy as long as I'm successful and others think well of me." Or "I don't have time to feel any of these feelings right now. Feelings just get in the way. I need to focus on performance, strategy, and action."

You might not have been conscious of that need to be accepted when you were little, but I bet if you look back now you can see some patterns beginning in your childhood.

And you are most likely beginning to see them now.

✎ So back to the workbook for questions that will take you deeper into your story to find more answers.

Eight - Fear:

As human beings we are born with a certain amount of natural fear. There are only two fears we come into the world with. The fear of falling and the fear of loud noises.

The rest are fears we learn as we grow up. We are taught what to fear through the filters of our parents, those we are in close contact with and our environment. Sometimes we learn them from listening, and sometimes from observing.

As children we cannot live with ambiguity, so we attach meaning to what we see and hear along the way. It doesn't matter what meaning we assign to those things. It just must make sense to us and then we go about living that truth until somewhere along the way we stop and reframe what ended up being a lie. We tell ourselves that somehow we must have caused the problem. If our mom and dad are constantly fighting, then somehow it must be me who is causing it and since I believe it's my fault then there must be something I can do to fix it. In this way I can feel like I have some control in my little life and therefore I won't have to be afraid.

If you are a perceptive child, you will learn to pick up on other's tensions and it will be simply by watching them. No one will need to tell you or explain it as you will gather up the energy just by being in the presence of it.

For example: My dad was sick all through my childhood and was hospitalized numerous times as I was growing up. My mom would take us to the hospital, and we would stand on the grass outside all the windows, while she pointed out which window to wave at. We were never allowed inside to see my dad. But all the times I stood there waving I could never see him, so I wasn't even sure he was there.

It was terribly confusing to a four-year-old because no one really spoke of what was happening and I was left to my own imagination to interpret why he was there, when he was coming home or if he would ever be better enough to walk back through the front door. It felt like my mom was keeping a secret and although I was too young to understand what wasn't being said I was a keen observer and that ended up adding to my own fear and discontent.

My mother carried the energy of terror with her. As the oldest in this family I became acutely aware of the ways she felt, and how she moved through the day and I interpreted the way in which she acted. She never let me out of her sight. We rarely had a babysitter, if ever. She was always in control of everything and everyone, so I took those behaviors to mean something was always wrong and I needed to stick close to her side.

Although my perception may have been off, it's how I made sense of my world and began to see life as scary and unpredictable.

The world became smaller and smaller and when it was time to go to school, I was convinced my mom was trying to get rid of me. Why would she keep me so tightly by her side and now leave me in a place I didn't know with people I didn't trust? I remember leaving the school grounds as a five-year-old and walking home from kindergarten to surprise her with "Hey mom, I'm home." I think she almost passed out.

By that time there were three of us and my brother and sister were home with her while I was exiled into a foreign land of school.

As a first grader it got even worse.

I vomited in the school yard every morning and had diarrhea each afternoon waiting for her to come pick me up. I recall telling the eighth grader who stood with me after the bell rang that my mom was never going to come get me. As I think back today, I feel such a sense of sadness for this child who had to grow up being terrified of abandonment at the age of six. That pattern of behavior grew as I did and as a young adult many of my unhealthy choices were prompted by my fear of being abandoned.

My mom finally took me to see a therapist and he told her if she didn't let go of her grip on me, she would cripple me forever.

Hyper vigilance became my daily coping mechanism and the fear of death lived with me each day until I sought help through my own work with a life coach.

There's no on and off on switch that I can flip to rid me completely of these old coping mechanisms and I still must deal with some irrational fears that show their ugly heads on occasion. The difference today is I don't fight them or get angry because they are here again. And pushing the feelings down or resisting them only make them worse. I choose to greet them and ask them why they are here. The answer is always the same.

They have come to remind me there is a God and He loves me. I can recognize them for what they are. Fear is a lie. It disrupts my peace and distracts me from the truth. I simply need to be still, call them out and then let them go. It's not easy to release such deeply embedded beliefs that have been my protector for so long, but as I become more mindful of living in the moment I am not as likely to go into my head and entertain thoughts that frighten me.

I am learning that not all the fear I feel belongs to me and that I can let go of the feelings I inherited from my family.

Without overthinking, write down in your workbook or journal some ideas that come to mind that might help you release your fears. It doesn't matter if they are doable or not. The intention is to begin writing whatever comes without judgment or criticism. It's a way to engage your brain into thinking about possibilities instead of limitations. You can look at your thoughts later but once you give yourself a chance to unlock what's being held in your mind it opens your mind and heart to other strategies and ideas.

✎ Take out your workbook and let's get to writing.

Nine - Procrastination:

If I have learned anything through my experience, it's that I may have an issue with procrastination, but I am not a procrastinator. We are not our patterns. We might have certain behaviors we'd like to be free of but those don't define who we are today.

We are so much more than what we do or don't do.

It's about who we BE in the middle of acknowledging our shortcomings and striving to do better with each new tool we gain along the path of life.

How many times have I had something I needed to do only to consciously seek something to distract me? How many times have I promised myself I wouldn't do that same behavior again only to find myself repeating the pattern over and over again while internally bashing myself for being so undisciplined?

While doing my research I came across a great article that explained some of the challenges that go with practicing the art of procrastinating.

This is from the blog of Amazing Marvin:

While from the outside laziness and procrastination can look the same, what is going on inside the people doing these things is fundamentally different.

Laziness is about not being willing to put in the work and energy needed to do something.

Whereas procrastination is about feeling unable to put in the work, despite really wanting to.

What is the difference between laziness and procrastination?

Laziness is a choice.

As strange as it may sound at first, laziness is a choice, in the sense that you don't want to put in the work or energy so you don't.

You might choose to have a lazy Sunday where you take it easy and don't do much.

A lazy person, despite its negative connotation, is simply a person who doesn't want to put a lot of extra work or effort into something (e.g. in life or their job).

Sometimes people also refer to being lazy as having a lack of energy or a feeling of tiredness.

You might say "I am feeling lazy today" when you feel a lack of energy. Being tired is of course not a choice (but perhaps a consequence of certain choices you have made) but we will get back to this later.

But isn't laziness a bad thing?

Laziness has a negative connotation because as a society we tend to want individuals to contribute as much as possible and being lazy is seen as a detriment to overall society.

But there are many cultures where being lazy (by other culture's standards) is accepted and even the norm. And while those societies might have a lower GDP, the people living there tend to be happier and live longer. Productivity is not the only value system.

In my opinion, if being lazy doesn't come at a large cost to others, there is absolutely nothing wrong with choosing a relaxed life where you avoid any extra effort or work. Everyone should live their life as they want. And life thrives on diversity.

So, while laziness might be seen as a problem by society or other people, it isn't seen as a problem by the lazy person themselves. That is the crucial difference between laziness and procrastination.

Procrastination is not a choice. As a procrastinator, you want to get lots of things done, but you feel unable to do so.

Many procrastinators describe having a strong inner resistance that feels like a barrier between them and the tasks at hand.

Procrastination at its core is a failure of self-regulation or more specifically, emotional regulation.

A task elicits a negative emotion (e.g. fear, boredom, frustration etc.) so the natural instinct is to avoid it.

While it is technically possible to go ahead and override this instinct, for a chronic procrastinator the emotions are often too strong to overcome.

In summary, with procrastination there is a disconnect between what you want to do and what you end up doing.

Therefore, procrastination leads to so many negative secondary feelings such as hopelessness, frustration with oneself, self-hatred and even depression.

Procrastinators tend to not be lazy.

What is interesting is that many procrastinators are very driven individuals and anything but lazy.

Procrastinators often have very high standards for themselves and ambitious goals they want to achieve.

This of course makes procrastination even more painful, and it can also be an underlying factor in why one struggles with procrastination in the first place.

Laziness vs. burnout

If you have started to feel "lazy" over time and are bothered by it, you might be suffering from burnout, depression, or another underlying health problem.

Laziness in this context refers to a general lack of energy (physical or mental) or a feeling of tiredness.

Am I lazy or procrastinating?

If you are bothered by your lack of activity, ask yourself what is the main thing holding you back:

Is it a feeling of dread, overwhelm, fear, a sense of inner resistance to getting started? Then you are likely suffering from procrastination.

Or is it a feeling of exhaustion, tiredness, mentally or physically where it feels like taking action is too much of a struggle that keeps you from taking action? Then your issue might be burnout or some other underlying health problem.

For most people suffering with chronic procrastination, it is a mix of these two things. Both are associated with long-term stress, so it is a positive feedback loop making all these issues worse.

If, on the other hand, you just tend to not be interested in doing certain things because you don't really see the point in doing them, then you might just be someone who has a different value system than the people around you. It is often other people or comparison to others that make us feel "lazy" or like our laziness is a problem

Ask yourself if you are OK with the level of effort you are putting into life and what you get out of it. If so, then carry on.

……. End of article.

Have you ever considered there might be benefits from your procrastinating? Or are you too blinded by your critical self-talk that you can't see any value in your how you put things off?

Maybe it's time to pause and look at some of the good that can come out of your hesitations.

1. You may work better under a restrictive deadline. Putting off something you should do now may give you time to do other things. You can put your attention on other possibilities for the time being and when the deadline gets near you get to work to complete the task.

2. Generally we procrastinate on things that bore us or don't bring us joy. As the end gets closer, we often get a boost of adrenaline and in that energy, we become more curious and motivated to get the job done. I believe I am an undiagnosed adult with ADD. My mom was told by a psychologist friend that when I was little, she considered me to be hyperactive. I was great at beginning but got so bored in between the starting line and the finish line I would simply walk away and start another project. As I matured, I looked at all the undone things in my wake and began to choose to not even begin because I was frustrated at my lack of focused attention to get anything done. Did I procrastinate because I ignored the value of getting the job done? I don't think

so and it wasn't until I could come up with a simple system that I could grasp a new way to complete the tasks ahead.

In Mary Kay there was something called "The Six Most Important Things" list. We were encouraged to write out the list at night before we went to bed of the things that needed our attention in the morning. We would then start with the most challenging chore first. When we completed that we crossed it off the list and moved on to number 2. And continued until the list was finished. When I used this exercise, I got so much more done and felt proud of myself for not leaving behind promises I had made to myself and forgotten along the way.

The list held my attention and made it easier for me to concentrate on the task at hand. However, I did need to be conscious of not making the list longer than six things and the tasks had to be achievable in the time frame I had during the day. Otherwise, it was a set up for me to fail and I'd completely abort the whole project because I was overwhelmed. When I keep that in mind, I find the process still works today.

3. When we put things off until there is no longer any time to waste, we grab onto our creativity to make it happen. We feel the challenge of the race to the finish line, and it jump starts new and creative ideas to make the end result amazing.

   Remember that not all patterns labeled ineffective or bad are really that. There are benefits to everything we do and it's how we choose to see these behaviors that will determine how we live them.

   Maybe procrastinating has caused you some heartache in the past. Maybe you feed on it. Whatever you choose it's your decision. What works best for you? Do not allow those who judge your behaviors to be the ones who make your decisions for you.

In the accompanying workbook you will see more questions about perfectionism and procrastination that may help you get a bit more clarification on how these might be interrupting your life and what to do next.

Ten - Scarcity Mind set.

What exactly is a scarcity mind set? From webmd.com the definition is:

"When you are so obsessed with a lack of something-usually money or time- that you can't seem to focus on anything else, no matter how hard you try."

Having a scarcity mind set can become a self-fulfilling prophecy. Because these beliefs make it difficult to move forward.

Is it learned or are we born with it? I think we all know the answer is this kind of mind set is caught in our childhood.

By caught I mean it's something we observe, hear, or interpret because no one sits us down as children and teaches us scarcity mindset 101.

I carried this mindset from early on. I remember hearing one or both of my parents saying," we don't have the money, or I don't have time." I was extremely perceptive, and I internalized much of what they did and then created a story in my mind to make sense of what I was watching.

As more children were born into our family (remember I am the oldest of five) I began to see how I had to give up more of my parents' time, energy, love, and attention for the next sibling that came along. I never felt like I got enough of them from the beginning because of my dad's alcoholism and now I was getting less. My belief was that somehow, I was unworthy, or they would have found a way to meet my needs.

As time progressed, I felt guilty for not being happy each time my mom told us she was pregnant. I was supposed to be, but I wasn't. I was completely confused because if they didn't have enough for the children they had, why on earth would they keep having more. I had no one to talk to and even if I did, I don't think I would have ever confessed I was resentful of having another brother or sister. Maybe I didn't even know how I felt, but I do recall not feeling warm and fuzzy about the whole ordeal.

I had heard or seen the same thing for many years. My mom was so exhausted raising us while dealing with an absent husband that she told me after I had grown up that she didn't have the capacity to love us. She gave us an education, home, and food but that was about all she could give.

From the beginning I had a feeling of not enough. I wasn't enough and there was never enough.

What I saw and heard growing up was not congruent.

I was afforded my education at a private girl's high school. I knew that was expensive so if we didn't have enough money how was I able to go to the school on the hill? Or how could we take road trips to Canada and North Carolina every other year?

The mixed messages were constant. I had no capacity to make sense of nonsense. I was confused and felt lost in a sea of irrational behavior.

As an adult I was attracted to those who continued to give mixed messages.

Boyfriends who said they cared about me but would stand me up on a date. Or arrive three hours late with no explanation when I greeted them at the door with a tear-stained face. Or going to the prom and watching my boyfriend order more than he could pay for and looking to me to pay the bill.

And I still sought out those who would validate my unworthiness. It was in my daily habits. I would promise myself, NEVER AGAIN, only to be right back in the same mess I just got myself out of.

Childhood coping skills are the same skills that create havoc in our adult lives. The way we do one thing is the way we do everything.

Here I am years later working my Mary Kay business trying to maintain production and wondering if those who say they are going to do what they promised are really going to follow through?

And then get angry and resentful when they don't. You see one of my biggest challenges has been the mindset that if you say you are going to do something it has become, in my mind, a promise. And people don't break promises. If they do, then I cannot trust them anymore.

Yet again, I confirm what I have always known to be true. No one can be trusted. People lie. They tell you only what you want to hear.

It is the same loop of lies I told myself as a kid and here I am today feeding the same lies.

These mind sets are created long before we could even speak.

We made sense out of nonsense and called it truth.

That's why it is so imperative to address our thinking before we can ever hope to see any outward change. It all begins in our heads. We hear it all the time.

What you think about you bring about. What am I thinking about without being aware? What is quietly moving through my subconscious that I am actively acting out with others?

It is worth it to take a look and see what's there.

You cannot fix what you don't know Is broken.

✎ Time to drop into your workbook and do some journaling.

FLUID

CHAPTER 2
Learning to:

One - Recognize my triggers.

Do you even know what your triggers are?

A trigger is a stimulus that elicits a reaction. It can be a word, a sound, the look on someone's face, a tone of voice. It can be a place that brings back a memory, good or bad. Even a taste or smell that brings forward a long-time memory you may have forgotten.

When we can recognize our triggers, it helps us to pause, breathe and pivot. We can assess the situation before we react. We can stop and regroup.

But if we have never looked at what the possibilities are before we are hit with those memories or physical sensations, we don't have time to think during a chaotic reaction that we can't stop.

When I am having an emotional overload episode it often happens when I am dealing with HALT.

> Hungry
> Angry
> Lonely
> Tired

Any of these feelings can trigger a reaction from me without even catching my breath.

And when you have spent your life burying your feelings they don't go away and are certainly not healed. They are just in hiding until something happens and an avalanche of feelings start rolling haphazardly towards those you love or maybe a total stranger.

For example, many years ago, when my children were small, my youngest son, Shawn, surprised my mom from behind by poking her in the sides.

She lost her marbles and her mind and screamed relentlessly at him until he dashed behind me and began to cry. He was so scared he could barely talk.

My thought was, what the heck?

I settled him down and then approached her. "Mom, what just happened?"

She told me she didn't like being poked or surprised because of something that happened in her childhood. I don't remember if she gave me more details, but I could tell she was not happy being touched in that way.

I told her I understood her discomfort but her reaction to her grandson was confusing and out of proportion for what he did. He didn't know she had issues from her childhood lurking under the surface of her smile. And because those memories and feelings had been shut away from the light and lived in her deep dark past, he suffered the consequences that belonged to someone else.

That's what happens when we don't do the work to heal where we have come from.

Do we know we need healing? Not always.

Do we know we have triggers? Maybe not.

But what I do know is when we have been hit with an experience that tells us there is more there to be discovered and possibly addressed the only person who can take responsibility and ownership of that is you.

No one can make another person seek help or look at what might be going on inside them, but they can set a boundary and choose to limit the time they spend with those they don't trust.

After seeing my son hurt, I had to decide what was best for all of us and then make the best decision for my family.

I think my mom went to counseling after what happened with Shawn and I'm grateful she was exposed to a pain that needed intervention, but the damage had been done to my child.

I believe we all have those moments when our old behaviors or triggers are exposed and then the question becomes, "Where do I go from here?"

For some, they choose to live in denial and say there is nothing wrong. It wasn't their fault. If only so and so hadn't done what they did, they would not have reacted.

When someone I love lives in denial, it is not my job to put their face in what they can't see. My only responsibility is to set my personal boundaries and live true to those.

What are my triggers?

The first one that seems to be the most challenging to let go of is my need to defend myself.

When I interpret someone's comments to be a criticism of me, I immediately find ways to let the accuser know why I did what I did and give them the reasons behind my actions or words.

I put up my dukes and take a fighting stance.

And yes, I know exactly where this comes from.

It began when I got punished for things in my childhood I didn't do and was given the belt as punishment.

I would try to explain to my dad what happened, but he would put his hand in front of my face and say, "Not another word." I would go ballistic inside. I never let my rage show but inside I was hysterical. I was so angry at my younger brothers and sister for having to take the abuse on their behalf that I could hardly contain my bitterness and resentment.

And retribution would follow.

It wasn't always like this. Sometimes they did get their punishment and when that happened, I would hide silently behind the big red chair, bundled into a human ball with my feet pulled up tightly under my chin and cry.

FLUID

I was torn between loving them and hating them.

The truth is I never hated my siblings, but I was sure frustrated with them.

Today when my husband or anyone accuses me of something I haven't done I am almost immediately back in time reacting in the same way I did when I was facing my father,

It's instant.

My fists are up, and my stance is fierce.

I know I am not going to be harmed because I am an adult and those days are long gone, but the reaction is rapid and strong.

As I become aware of the voice that is lying and whispering I am not safe, I can tell it to STOP.

I can take a breath.

I can center myself.

I can say a prayer for peace.

And I can observe what is happening in the moment that is creating such havoc inside me.

I can assess the situation and then respond accordingly.

However, what I don't have to do anymore is "JADE."

I don't have to justify, argue, defend, or explain my decisions, my beliefs, my feelings, or my thoughts, unless I choose to.

I don't have to be bullied by anyone to ease their pain by owning what isn't mine. Saying I am sorry for something I haven't done, or making sure I help them understand so they won't take their aggression or frustration out on me.

Each of us is responsible for our own actions. And when we can see what triggers us, we can avoid overreacting and saying something mean spirited and hurting others.

We are not perfect and there will be times when what we say and do might hurt someone. It is then that I can say I am sorry they were hurt by what I said and did. But if I know that what I said was truthful, kind, and respectful and they just choose to be angry, then they have some work to do as well.

I can apologize because they are feeling pain, but I don't have to say I am sorry for their misinterpretation of what I said.

✎ Please take out your workbook and look over the questions. They might give you some perspective on how your triggers are affecting you in your everyday life.

Two - How to stop "shoulding "on myself and others

The definition of should is this:

Used to indicate obligation, duty, or correctness, typically when criticizing someone's actions.

The shoulds come from the voice of the judge that lives in our heads.

He shows up in every chapter of this book and every chapter of our lives.

He is there from morning to night.

He is loud and he is quiet.

He is harsh and critical.

And he is constant and unrelenting.

We all have the voice of the judge. It can be the voice of society and unhealthy leaders.

It speaks up when we aren't comfortable in our own skin. It speaks when we feel less than. It offers judgment not only to us but to others and circumstances as well.

When we doubt our value, the judge reinforces the idea that we really are unworthy. Like "Who do you think you are?

No one wants to hear what you have to say. You are getting too big for your britches." It's the voice from our past. Maybe it was our parents or a teacher or friend who planted a seed that we are not okay being who we are and we SHOULD be someone else.

You know the dialogue. You should try harder. You should be a good girl. You should be more generous. You should be more focused and then you will do better. Should, should, should.

Often when I hear that voice, I recognize it as my mom's when she was tired and frustrated and she needed me to be invisible and silent so she could think. She was doing the best she had with the tools, ideas, and beliefs she had learned and carried forward with her into adulthood.

Whenever she was having trouble feeling comfortable in her own skin her voice would become harsh and critical.

This realization makes me wonder what my voice sounded like in the ears of my children when I was frustrated, lonely, angry, and tired.

What voices do they carry in their heads that belong to me?

And how can I make amends for the harm I caused when I was just trying to live in the midst of my own sorrow and pain?

It might be a good time to sit with my adult children who are now parents and talk about this very subject.

How do we stop doing this to ourselves and those around us?

We call out that voice. We make it a third person and speak to that voice as though it is coming from outside of us rather than inside. WE stop when we hear those statements and say, "Oh there you are judge. You are a liar and what you speak no longer holds the truth for me. I choose to let go of what you're saying because I know who I am, and I am good enough."

Those around me and my situations don't need my criticism. They need my acceptance.

Today I know accepting others doesn't mean I approve of what they're doing, and it doesn't mean I stand in judgment either. It simply means I need to let them and my current circumstances be, and if necessary, set appropriate boundaries.

Keep in mind how you feel when someone tells you "You should." That helps when it comes to our judgment of those we love.

Also, when we pass judgment on our circumstances, it only makes living through them more difficult, and we end up taking on the mindset of a victim rather than addressing the situation with a more proactive stance.

So when you hear the voice again, because you will hear it over and over, take a breath and do your PQ reps.

You remember we spoke of this a few chapters back.

FLUID

Close your eyes. Gently run two fingers together with such tension you can feel the fingertip ridges on both fingers. Do that for at least twenty seconds. Breathe and let go.

✎ Workbook time.

Three - Stay in your own hula hoop.

What I really mean is mind your own business.

That's a tough one for sure. I think we are conditioned to believe if we care about someone, we need to help them even if they don't ask. And we need to worry. The amount of worry determines the amount of love we have for them. NOT!!!!

It's easier to pay attention to you than it is to make my own personal changes. I can help you far quicker than I can help myself. At least that's the lie I feed myself and then believe.

I remember all the times I was worried about my children who suffered from the disease of addiction. I was afraid they would do something that might harm them or others. Thinking about them became a full-time job.

They were constantly bombarding my mind with fearful thoughts I couldn't control. I felt obsessed with making sure they were safe. I knew I couldn't keep functioning like this. I was restless. I couldn't focus. I didn't sleep. I was distracted all the time and began feeling resentful of their behavior because THEY were making my life unbearable.

The truth is I was choosing to be consumed with thoughts of them. They didn't have a clue and didn't really care about how their behavior or life choices were affecting me. After all, they didn't ask me to worry.

I was their mother, and I was responsible for them and their wellbeing. Until I wasn't.

It wasn't my job to get my teenagers up and ready for school in the morning. Or make sure they had their breakfast. Or drive them the mile to school. They could use an alarm clock. They could make their own pieces of toast. They could walk or ride a bike to school. They could figure it out.

But only if I let go of my grip so they could.

I was scared. I believed I was helping them.

But all I was doing was hindering them from developing the life skills they needed to move on when they finished high school.

As I began to give them the responsibility of taking care of themselves and their own needs, I felt cold-hearted. I believed my new behavior was mean and brisk. My heart was hurting. I was afraid they would think I didn't love them.

But I also felt used and unappreciated. I gave my everything only to have them wanting more. I was exhausted and blamed them.

After seeking my own counsel and starting to make my own course corrections I began to back away and stopped offering unsolicited advice. You see, every time I gave them suggestions they didn't seek, I was slowly becoming the enemy.

And although they started pulling away it wasn't because they wanted to learn to become healthier adults. It was because they were starting to hate me and my meddling in their affairs.

Yes, I was responsible for them until they turned 18 but I was not responsible to get them to work, or make sure their homework was done. Or that they got to school on time. I was to make sure they were loved, fed, and cared for.

What I had to discover on this journey was the heartache and pain I was trying to soothe by taking overly good care of them wasn't theirs. It was mine.

If they didn't do what they were supposed to do, then they would reap the consequences. When I had to watch them suffer for the choices they made, it hurt me. I didn't want to feel my own pain around their choices so I would do everything I could to help them avoid making those mistakes.

In the end, all that did was postpone the inevitable and make us all unhappy.

I made a lot of errors along the way. Two steps forward and one step back but eventually I was able to detach my heart strings from theirs and give them the grace and space they needed to grow.

It was more about me than about them.

I had to make friends with my heartache. I had to wrap my arms around me when the grief hit so hard I thought I'd lose my footing. I had to cry out to God to help me breathe through these life contractions.

I had to be willing to own my own personal sadness and grief to give my children the freedom to embrace their own sorrow and heartache. Stepping out of their hula hoop was the hardest lesson I have ever learned.

Last year I was given the opportunity to host a women's retreat in Sedona with eight beautiful souls from all over California and Arizona.

It was a magical weekend with so much love, laughter, tears, and healing.

I decided to bring an actual hula hoop with me and one night when we were finished with dinner, I asked for a volunteer to step into the hula hoop with me.

Terry graciously accepted and together we bumped around trying to fit in one hula hoop.

Who was going to oversee which way we spun? Who was going to control the rhythm of the moves?

Well, I bet you can guess those answers.

No one.

It was hysterical and we laughed so hard we almost peed our pants.

It was impossible for either of us to be comfortable or content in one hula hoop and everyone could visually see the importance of staying out of one another's business when it comes to loving and accepting our fellow human beings.

✎ Grab your workbook and start writing.

Four- Setting stronger boundaries.

Boundaries are important.

They are necessary to live a healthy life with ourselves and others.

But they are scary to set, and it takes courage to set them.

No one wants to be rejected and that's the greatest fear we face when we say No, or that's enough, or your behavior and words are not okay with me. In the end, owning our truth and speaking it gives us a sense of freedom we may have never felt up until that point of speaking up.

We learn by watching and listening. But most often it's the watching that influences us most.

I was extremely diligent when it came to observing my surroundings and the people living in my home. I listened intently and monitored everything.

One of the things I did NOT learn growing up was the idea of boundaries. No one in our family knew where one person ended and the other one began. We were constantly in each other's business and most of the time we were crammed in one another's hula hoops to the point of feeling like sardines in a crowded tin.

We told each other's business to anyone who would listen. My story was her story, and her story was my brother's story until the emotional waters were so muddy no one could see or feel clearly anymore. It was complicated, messy, and confusing. We were frequently frustrated with one another and there was virtually no peace in our home.

I remember finding out my sister was pregnant with her first child and when I spoke with my grandmother, I was so excited for my sister that I shared her good news with her. Before my sister could.

When she called my grandma so filled with joy, she was told her news was old news as I had already spilled the beans. My sister was heartbroken, and I felt horrible. You see, it wasn't my news to tell.

This is what happens when there are no boundaries to set limits in place.

I didn't think sharing family business was a big deal until I heard her voice of disappointment.

This moment in time changed how I thought about what I did. I was guilty. Now what?

Although I am aware of the damage I caused that day, one would think I learned to never speak out of turn again. Nope. That's not my story. There have been many times since when I opened my mouth, before thinking, and stuck both feet in.

But with each faux pas I am given the chance to rethink how I am going to share news of my family and I choose to let other's business be theirs. But I also want to recognize that my business belongs to me.

I will never forget when I told a friend my mom had passed away and before I could share it openly, it was posted on Facebook by someone else. The friend had told another friend and she decided it was hers to tell so she made my news public before I was ready.

I knew she didn't intend for her announcement to be hurtful, but it was, and I will always remember how I felt to see it before I could even take a breath.

Before we speak, or post or share we would be better off if we sought clarity and permission from the one who holds the story.

In reading the book of Numbers in our Bible study this past summer I learned some things.

God is the creator of boundaries and refuge. God established the boundaries within the promised land to provide protection, productivity, flourishing and sustainability.

"Boundaries" provide a framework to determine who or what to let in and who or what to keep out. The 10 Commandments are boundaries.

Boundaries were never meant to be walls. God never intended for us to shut out the world. We need to have discernment. Boundaries create balance. God doesn't want us to shun others because we're angry or disappointed. He really wants healing in relationships but not at the detriment of our own physical, emotional, and spiritual well-being.

One of the biggest boundaries I ever set and by far the scariest was with my parents. They were coming up on their 50th wedding anniversary and had asked us, their five children, to set up and pay for a party to celebrate them.

We all agreed and went about trying to find a place and menu that could accommodate not only their needs and desires but our pocketbooks as well.

We ended up confirming the rec center at their new living place and were excited to make arrangements for everyone planning on flying in to honor them.

One afternoon my mom called us to tell Joe, my husband, happy birthday and to catch up on what had been accomplished so far. She shared that she had invited my ex-husband (my kid's dad) and his wife to the party. And he had accepted and was coming.

I was shocked and Joe, on the other phone, was speechless.

When we hung up we looked at one another with our mouths open and had a hard time finding words to explain exactly how we felt.

This was the man who had walked out on me with another woman. He rarely saw his children and fought me tooth and nail in paying his child support.

He bad mouthed me to our children and when I would come up to visit the kids after they had relocated to Washington and he would tell the kids he didn't want me stepping anywhere in HIS state. He would go hunting each time I went north. I laugh about it now but when it was happening it hurt my heart. He was a hunter and I found it interesting that he always had an itchy trigger finger when I was coming.

I felt angry and betrayed. I was confused as to why my mom and dad wanted the man who had treated their daughter so poorly to attend their anniversary celebration.

All I knew, in that moment, was I couldn't control who they invited but

I could definitely set a boundary and choose not to attend a gathering where my former abuser would be sharing space.

I called my mother and asked her and my father to meet with us. I told her I didn't want to meet at either of our homes or at a public restaurant and we settled on a park located in between our cities. She made the comment that she felt like she was going to the principal's office, and I responded, "This is not going to be easy."

Fearful that I wouldn't be able to tell them how I felt, I chose to write it out in a letter and read it to them. This would ensure I could stay on task and not get sidetracked by their responses.

I simply stated if he were to come, I would not.

I was scared to death to speak up and tell them how I was feeling as I always went along with whatever they wanted. It was easier to go with the flow than to rock the boat and experience their emotional and physical rejection.

I asked them why they felt the need to invite him in the first place. I think it was more my mom's idea than my dad's because my mom cried more when my husband walked out than I did.

That always confounded me.

Anyway, I asked her if my ex called her and kept up with her? She said no. Did he come to visit? No. Did he make any attempts to keep the relationship alive and well? No.

Then what?

Why?

She said because when they went to Washington to see their grandchildren, he would take them to nice restaurants for dinner.

Before we left the park my dad told me he felt like he was being taken hostage. I said he could invite anyone he wanted, and I wasn't trying to control anyone's choices.

I was making a decision to care for my needs and protect myself from a man who had repeatedly hurt me in the past.

I was no longer willing to "Suck it up, buttercup."

They were as shocked with my new behavior as I was with their old.

It didn't take long for my mom to reach out to me and say she had called my ex-husband and requested he not come. If she had to choose between him or me, she would choose me.

I was grateful but sad that the experience had to happen at all.

Our family gathered with adult children, husbands and wives, significant others, extended family, and friends and had a wonderful party. Everyone had a beautiful time together.

After the party my dad didn't speak to me for four months. He was silent and distant. My mother did her best to stay connected, but it was tedious and stressful as the days and weeks passed.

I never regretted my decision. I was tired of betraying myself to make others happy.

My parents blamed my husband for the decision because they didn't think I was strong enough to make it on my own.

They were wrong.

After those few months went by my mom called to say my dad wanted to meet for lunch.

I was hesitant and told her so.

She said she thought it would be a good idea to meet him halfway and hear what he had to say.

I was uncomfortable with the idea. I didn't trust him.

He was an angry man when I was little. What would make him any different now?

But I felt the nudge of the Holy Spirit and said yes to lunch.

We met at an Olive Garden off the 91 freeway in between Costa Mesa and Riverside and when I pulled into the parking place, he was standing outside with a long stem rose in his hand.

I got out of the car, and we greeted one another. He gave me the rose and I noticed it had no thorns on it.

I said, "Dad, there are no thorns on this rose."

He smiled and replied, "I know. No more thorns."

We went inside, got a table and over lunch he asked for my forgiveness for having been so insensitive to my feelings. We both cried and on that day our relationship reached a newer and deeper level of healing.

We could have missed it if I "just went along" like I always did.

And because I chose to gather my courage and be open and honest, we gave each other freedom to move forward in a healthier and happier way.

Boundaries?

Hard to set? Yes.

Necessary? Yes

Worth it?

Absolutely.

✎ Time to go and review the questions in your workbook. Answer as honestly as you can and try not to overthink.

Five - Letting go of the voices of judgment I carry.

As we discussed briefly before, we all carry the voice of judgment in our heads.

It's something we learned along the way of life. If we had critical parents who told us we needed to do more to live up to their expectations, teachers who told us we weren't living up to our full potential (who ever lives up to their potential in grades 1-12) boyfriends who said they'd love us more if we would just lose a few pounds, or friends who told us to stop complaining, we heard the voice of judgment all around us, all the time.

Soon their voices of criticism became ours and we began to live a truth that was never ours from the beginning.

It's the voice who speaks of our mistakes by labeling us as the mistake. We can't do anything right. We are too hopeless to even dream of a better life and if we do, who do we think we are that we'd deserve one. If we were proud of an accomplishment, we were too big for our britches, conceited and stuck up.

That voice is a liar. It has fed us untruths for long enough and it has convinced us that it means well. And that it's our friend.

WRONG!!!

The messages it feeds us are things like:

1. Without me pushing you, you will be lazy or complacent.
2. Without me punishing you for your mistakes, you will never learn.
3. Without scaring you about bad future outcomes, you will not work hard enough to prevent them.
4. Without me judging others you will lose your objectivity and not protect yourself.
5. Without me making you feel bad, you will do nothing to change it.

(the five statements above are taken from Shirzad Charminne and positiveintelligence.com)

All feelings of guilt, shame, regret, disappointment, anger and anxiety are directly connected to the judge.

I often reflect on why I am so quick to judge others. I know I am blessed and am grateful for all I have, but it's almost a default to look at others and instantly criticize them.

It's usually stems from jealousy. When you have something I don't or can't have or you are doing something I can't do, the judge comes charging with both barrels drawn. I am angry you have what I can't. It has to do with my own personal limitations, or it could be circumstances that might be preventing me from doing what you are doing in the way that brings you great success.

I find myself having a pity party or a temper tantrum and then I decide, in my head, you have done something wrong or unethical to have what you have.

I have completely fallen off my emotional cliff and the voice of God has gone mute. Even if He was screaming the blessings He has given me, I am too caught up in my head to even hear Him.

I am believing the lies of the judge.

You don't deserve what you have.

You cheated to get where you are.

You had help no one else had.

I think you get my point.

I feel vulnerable sharing this raw and ugly truth with you, but those thoughts are there.

Not all the time.

But they still rise up when I am feeling less than. Not good enough. Disappointed in my choices or exhausted from living in the space I am living in.

They come roaring in without warning.

Although there are some things I am becoming aware of that could be triggers for me.

Scrolling social media when I am bored can create a tsunami of feelings about my worthiness.

Too much television can cause me to get on the comparison band wagon.

Eating an overabundant amount of sugar and not getting enough rest can also cause me to lose sight of what I am grateful for and thus end up headfirst in a cesspool of negative thinking.

It is ongoing but we can get better if we become conscious of what we are thinking that feeds what we are doing.

We do have choices and when we walk out of the emotional fog and into more light, we awaken to behaviors we have been doing for a lifetime that no longer serve us or those we love.

With this new awareness we can pause, take a deep breath and pivot to new and healthier choices.

Here are some simple ideas on how to embrace new ways of living.

1. Pause, breathe, and pivot. Take a minute to remember who you are. Not who the world is labeling you.
2. Imagine talking to a child in this moment and how would you communicate with them from a place of kindness and love. You wouldn't badger or berate them so why do that to yourself.
3. Acceptance is key to living a life of freedom. It is what it is. They are who they are. Acceptance doesn't mean approving of others' behaviors. It means we stop fighting to change what we can't and surrender knowing that letting go of what we are powerless to do is the only answer. Stop beating our heads against the wall and focus on what we can do to improve the situation without the need to control the outcomes.
4. It is only then that we can be clear headed enough to do the next indicated step in front of US.

✎ Time to move over to your workbook.

Six - Replace fear with faith.

Faith over fear is not an easy shift when fear has been growing in you since you were a kid. It has taken root inside you and a quick pluck won't get to the roots. It will take more than a simple release of this old behavior to be rid of it. At least that has been my experience.

Step five of the 12 steps in AA says, "Admitted to God, to ourselves, and to another human being the exact nature of our wrongs."

Step six says, "Were entirely ready to have God remove my shortcomings."

Step seven, 'Humbly ask Him to remove our shortcomings."

Here I am having openly admitted my defects of character to myself and another human being, God. Now I am ready for all those to be removed. NOW.

That's not how it works.

It takes time for whatever baggage we are carrying from the past to be released.

We might be all in to have God release it from us but maybe HE is not ready.

I heard once that God may use my defects to help others and in so doing, He won't set me free until His timing is perfect. Not necessarily for me but for Him and His purposes.

I recall feeling so filled with fear I could hardly see straight. I begged God to free me of this character defect because it was causing me so much pain and difficulty. I didn't want to live in my anxiety anymore. But even though I was desperate to be rid of it, He wasn't ready. I thought there must have been more for me to learn in this place.

What I discovered was humility. I didn't want anyone to know how I was feeling. Being afraid of dying seemed ridiculous and stupid. I am an adult, and I shouldn't be this way. I was sure I was the only one and I carried shame around this. I was embarrassed. I held my secret close to my chest and didn't disclose it to anyone other than my husband.

FLUID

We are only as sick as our secrets. When it got too heavy to keep hiding, I decided to be vulnerable and let others in. What I found is there were many who were holding the same secret and now they had someone they could relate to. We all felt the same way and now they could release their shame because they weren't alone.

God used my character defect to help others and that's why He didn't take it from me when I was so desperate for it to be gone.

For me it all comes down to faith. And learning to make friends with my fear. When I can recognize fear is merely a gift that draws me closer to God then I can more easily greet it, embrace it, be grateful for its arrival and let it go.

✎ Take out your workbook and continue with the questions.

Seven - Letting B- be good enough.

What? I could never let any grade be good enough other than an A.

"Why?" I ask. What does getting an A on every test or every class or every subject in school mean for you?

Success?

Perfection?

A great college?

A better job?

The right future?

Are you sure it's what it means to YOU or is it what your parents want for you?

And whose definition are you living?

Could it possibly be you are living out the generational expectations of those who lived before you?

I am not saying that A's are not a good thing. I'm just suggesting that when a B- cannot be accepted as good enough we carry that mindset way beyond school, and it can be a set up for major stress and frustration for the rest of your life.

A couple of years ago my husband and I went to visit my brother and his family in Palo Alto, CA. While we were there, he shared a story about the highschoolers and the expectations that had been put upon them by family and friends.

It seems it became necessary to provide 24-hour guards at the train crossings because there'd been an increase in suicides among young kids struggling to measure up. It made me pause and check in with how we, as people and society, can put our expectations of achievements we've never accomplished onto our children so they can make us proud.

And maybe what that does is create in them a pressure to perform beyond what they are capable of doing.

Maybe it sets them up to obtain things that are not important to them, and they end up chasing accomplishments that were never theirs to begin with.

Maybe it tells them what they really want is not important or vital to the path God has chosen for them.

Maybe they go through school cheating to get the grades and recognition you never got in high school.

Or maybe they spend their entire life doing what they hate because they were never encouraged to be who THEY are and seeking what they value.

When we live vicariously through others, we put our unmet goals and dreams on them rather than on ourselves, and we help create miserable people who never trust what they know.

I do recall when I was in grammar school, I was paid a dime for every A and had to pay my dad a nickel for every C. There weren't many words, but the message was clear. Mediocre was not acceptable and in order to be seen and heard in my family A's were where the money and attention was.

And in order to keep up the ruse that A's were all that were accepted I cheated on my tests to keep the image alive. I am not proud to admit that, but I did learn that being an authentic B- or C+ is better than a fake A.

And today I am still learning that being ME is much better than being a phony version of what someone else expects me to be.

✎ Time to turn to your workbook and check out your next set of questions.

Eight- Accepting who I am, where I am, as I am.

How do I do that?

How do I accept who I am today when I have made so many poor choices in the past?

How do I forgive myself for mistakes that seem so stupid when I look back?

I believe that nothing happens in our lives by accident.

There is a reason for every choice we've made and although it may seem ridiculous that we could even make those choices, it was meant to either teach us something or help us in our life's journey.

Many years ago, when I was married to my first husband and had a young son, my husband would invite his best friend over to the house for dinner and then he wouldn't come home. He would go to the local bar to drink while his friend was at our home paying attention to me.

Wrong choice on his part.

Being married to a workaholic, alcoholic left me feeling bitter, angry, and lonely.

When this man would come for dinner, he would pour attention all over me telling me how beautiful I was. How if I were his wife he would never neglect or abandon me.

It didn't take long to feed my desperate hunger to be seen and loved and you guessed it. I ended up in his arms in the middle of the day at a local motel with my car hidden on the side of the place where we secretly met.

I was a hot mess. I hid my secret for as long as possible until the day I was late on my period and had to tell my husband the truth about the possibility of me being pregnant.

My period started the following day, but the cat was out of the bag.

We ended up working things out and soon were transferred to California from Washington where we tried to put the broken pieces of our marriage back together.

I look back today and no longer carry the shame of being a cheating wife.

It was not the right thing to do. I knew that then but my hunger for love and affection took over my ability to think it through rationally.

Many might not believe this, but I know from learning about the disease of alcoholism, it's a family disease and we are all affected.

Everyone suffers and most of the time it's done in secret and in hiding.

I can see the heartache and sorrow I lived with daily as the broken wife of a man with a drinking problem. I have forgiven myself for not making better decisions. I could only do what I could do.

God has used my choice many times since to teach me compassion for other wounded women who are going through a time when they feel there is no other choice than to betray themselves.

It breaks my heart to see women squash their voices, shut off speaking their truth, and hide their brilliant light because of fear of another's reactions.

That's why I do what I do today.

To help them find their true, authentic voice and speak it loud and clear.

We are who we are because of each experience we have lived through since the day we were born.

Nothing happens TO us but rather FOR us.

We are the ones who get to take the discovery journey and put the pieces back together to create a beautiful picture of where we have travelled.

We are who we are and if we want to change who that person is today, we get to seek the help we need.

I have often heard the statement, "My children's problems may have my name on them, but their solutions have their name on them."

My parents did the best they could with the tools they had.

I did the same.

And my children are also doing the best they can.

Some days it's an awful sight.

But other days it's better.

One day at a time.

I cannot accept who I am today without forgiving the past version of who I was. This forgiveness allows me the ability to forgive others as well.

However, healing takes time.

It requires us to circle back to the pain and do more unpacking.

What is mine?

What is theirs?

Where do I need to extend my hand and ask for forgiveness and when do I make space and offer grace so others can reach out to me?

How do I let go of bitterness for the harm put upon me?

I am where I am today because of the choices I have made.

If I want to be somewhere else that's on me. I need to decide and then act on it. If I'm not ready, I am not ready.

"What now" you might be thinking?

Where do I go from here?

I go quiet when I am in a state of uncertainty.

I seek God's guidance through prayer and meditation.

I keep the process simple.

Listen.

FLUID

I do the next indicated step.

And I ask for help.

✎ You got it. Time for the workbook.

CHAPTER 3

Understanding: who I am.

One - Childhood memories

Sometimes I wonder how any of us survived our childhoods. And when it comes to memories how far back can we even remember?

I have heard many say they cannot remember anything and others that cannot forget.

I'm somewhere in the middle.

I am the product of each collective experience I have lived during my lifetime. The challenge is that I am the one who labeled each experience as good or bad. And that's exactly how I carried the lessons with me.

One memory I still carry with me was when I was two years old and lived in Venice Beach, California at the Lincoln apartments. We lived upstairs and I was often cared for by the eldest daughter of our neighbors who lived directly below us.

I woke up one morning to the sound of sirens and they were loud and close.

I don't know if I was able to get down the stairs by myself or if my mom took me outside to see what the disruption was all about.

There were police cars, firetrucks, and an ambulance in the car port area right behind the laundry room and I could see everything.

What I observed was a man being carried out on a stretcher with blood all over him and paramedics rushing to get him into the waiting ambulance.

His daughter was beside him heading to the ambulance as well and I was so curious about what had happened because I knew these neighbors.

I'm not sure how well I could know them since I was so small, but we were a tight knit group of neighbors and our families looked out for one another. I heard later, many years later the man had fallen through a glass shower door. I don't remember anything else about that.

Did he live?

Did he ever come home?

Did I see him again?

I can't answer those questions, and my parents are gone so I can't ask them what happened.

All I know is that up to a year or so ago, my spirit was getting startled by the sounds of sirens.

That sound triggers trauma and it only takes a second for me to be that little girl again standing helplessly in front of my apartment wondering what happened and how anyone was going to fix the man next door.

As I continue to do my own personal exploration work in my coaching practice, the more I am able to investigate and heal the wound of that trauma. But it is not an easy fix and cannot be addressed unless it can be recalled and looked at.

That's what I love about coaching. I come alongside women to help them find what continually hurts their hearts and souls and to discover ways to release and let go without discounting and shutting off the memory.

Throughout my growing up years it was me who gave meaning to things that didn't make sense. When my mom, who never left me with a babysitter, told me it was time to go to school (kindergarten) I was sure she was trying to get rid of me, and her plan was to never come pick me up. Instead, she would stay home with my siblings and care for them.

What made me think like that as a five-year-old? Maybe it was because she kept me so close for the first five years that when it was time for her to leave me in an unknown place, having had no prior experience of being left with anyone, I didn't know how to trust she would be back. The only thing left to my little mind was that I had done something terribly wrong and I deserved to be left behind.

And it continued into my early years at elementary school. Throwing up in the school yard before the bell rang and nausea and diarrhea at the end of the day.

It was awful and my mother had no clue what to do with me.

Eventually, I was taken to a counselor. I still remember the white building with the white stairs on the outside which we climbed to get to his office.

I sat on his stupid couch while he threw a dumb rubber ball at me wanting to play catch. My mom sat outside the door. I wasn't going for it and refused to play. When he asked if I wanted a soda, my response was, "Could my mom come?"

It was later in my life my mom shared that the therapist told her she needed to let go of me, or my spirit would die.

I have no clue how a terrified mother could do that, but somewhere along the way she began to ease up. However, for many years I looked at my world as not a safe place to live. The damage was done, and it would take a lifetime to undo what was so ingrained in me as a child.

I carried her fear with me.

Last year while working with my own personal coach, I was asked what my relationship with my abusive dad was like.

My life growing up with a crazy, angry alcoholic was not easy and I carried the scars with me being attracted to and marrying wounded men, just like him.

One example we spoke of was about his love of money over his love of me.

She was curious about that and asked some thought-provoking questions.

One was, "tell me more."

Well, when I was 21 and had decided to move with my newly divorced boyfriend to Montana for his new job as a Marine Corps. recruiter my dad told me we should get married.

Married? Why? I didn't want to be married to him. I just wanted to get away from my crazy and dysfunctional family home and this was my perfect way out.

My dad continued to tell me that if we were involved in a car accident along the way he wouldn't pay for my health care needs or the costs of the accident since I was no longer on his insurance.

"What? He wouldn't help me if I needed him."

It was then made very clear to me that he loved money more than he loved me.

But the seed of fear had been planted, so I told my boyfriend we better get married so I would have insurance.

Off to the Santa Ana City center to obtain a marriage certificate, celebrate in a civil wedding ceremony, a dozen roses and $100 from my parents and off to Montana we went.

By the way, when my husband filed for divorce 10 years later my only question was, "What am I going to do about insurance?"

Back to my coach's questions.

She then asked me if there may have been another motive behind what my dad had suggested. There was no other reason he would say what he said. But she told me to go along with her and see what I could come up with.

I sat silent for a long time and then spoke, "It could have been that he didn't want me to have an accident along the way and start out my life with this man in such financial debt I wouldn't see the light of day for a long time and would be financially responsible for many years to come?"

She agreed and asked if that was the story how would I feel?

"Well, if that was why, I would feel loved and cared for by my dad."

She was quiet.

I began to cry.

I had never given any kind of thought to the idea that my dad may have loved me so much he would want me protected.

She told me what we had just done was called a "Reframe." And she shared that the power of interpretation can change the trajectory of our lives.

It really didn't matter why my dad said what he said. It was more important how I took what he said and labeled it. Because how I interpreted it was how I would live it.

The first way made me feel like a victim and the second way made me feel loved.

There were so many times I interpreted other's behaviors as proof of my unworthiness. That I deserved to be abandoned or that there was something so intrinsically wrong with me I couldn't be loved for who I was.

There was never any real proof other than how I looked at the experiences and formed a belief about myself based on my childhood understanding. The only problem with that was I took that understanding into my adult life and continued to view it as truth.

It never dawned on me that I carried such deeply embedded old ideas that I reacted to my daily circumstances automatically, not aware I was in reaction mode.

I learned that I could let go of the hold those beliefs had on me. But I couldn't release them until I could replace them.

And reframing was the tool necessary to move on into healthier patterns of behavior.

My dad died four years before I experienced this life shift. But afterward I was able to forgive him for all the times he had physically and emotionally abused me and forgive myself for always choosing to see me in a victim role even when I knew it wasn't true anymore.

There are many more examples of childhood memories that have had a significant impact on who I am today. Many of those I have been given an opportunity to unpack, look at through a different lens, and make appropriate and healthy changes around them.

They will never be forgotten, but they will be appreciated as a gift of learning rather than a burden to be resented.

✎ Let's take some time to dive into our workbooks.

- Just a quick reminder. It's ok not to be ok and to ask for help when you're not.

Two- My own perfectly written novel

This technique was taught through PositiveIntelligece.com which was a yearlong training course I took to further my ongoing coaching education.

Everything that has happened along the road of my life has been preparing me for where I am now. Nothing has ever been random or haphazard. It has all been perfectly designed for the lessons I have needed to learn.

Those who have a spiritual practice may know this without any hesitation. The idea is that you are living and trusting in the grand design of your life. Others might find it hard to believe that this road was designed especially for each one of us.

It's okay if you don't. It's a self-fulfilling prophecy. You live your life based on the beliefs you have.

Nevertheless, we are all on a journey to learn and grow from each experience.

Regardless of your belief system, what if you chose to look at your life with the notion that every aspect of your life has happened for a reason?

What if your life is the perfectly written novel designed and written by the perfect novelist where the hero has lived through each chapter without any of the chapters being wasted?

Would you see the rest of your life a bit differently if you knew you could write new chapters and make better choices?

Let's explore this idea together.

You game?

I'd like to divide your life up by years into 5 chapters. For example. If you're 50 divided by 5 that equals 10. You would divide your life into chapters from age 0-10, 10-20, 20-30, 30-40 and 40-50.

If you're 65, divided by 5 the chapters would be 13-year increments.

If you're 40, divided by 5, you have chapters of 8 years each.

Got it?

Sit with your back straight, feet on the floor and close your eyes. Take a deep breath. Let go of any thoughts you might be having. Release the need to analyze any of what you're doing and just listen to your body as we do this contemplation.

Let's think of the first chapter of your life. If you're 50, it's the chapter between 0-10.

What were the highlights that you can remember?

If there was trauma, don't focus on that, but rather notice it.

What were the formative things that happened?

Words spoken? Actions taken? Family outings?

Ideas taught?

Beliefs shared?

Be aware of the situations that may have caused some distress, but don't open those up. Just notice they are there.

So, what were the gifts in terms of knowledge or strength that you gained in this chapter?

What did you learn about yourself as a youngster or about others? What did you learn about life?

Is there a name you'd like to give this chapter? Or a theme you see popping up?

Now let's move to the second sequence of years. What did you experience in this part of your life? The teenage years. What were the most memorable things or highlights you can recall? What did you learn that you may have brought forward into your current life today?

As you continue with each segment, write down what comes to mind.

With each segment the exercise is the same.

What do you remember?

What were the highlights or challenges during this time?

What feelings were consistent with each chapter?

What were the gifts of knowledge and understanding you received from each part of your novel?

As you complete the final chapter which brings you to your current age, give yourself a few minutes to rest your mind and your pen.

Take a few minutes to refresh your coffee or add ice to your water.

Breathe deeply.

Maybe take a walk and then come back for just one more exercise.

We are going to address one more chapter. We have called it the "Covid" chapter.

This chapter you've lived in and out of for the last few years. It may just be one of the most enlightening chapters of the life of our country.

Since the virus hit, what has been the greatest discovery you've learned or the biggest Ah Ha moment you have had? Maybe you have had many.

In this chapter, please list what you would consider the gifts.

What did you find out about who you are? What changes came in your relationship with yourself, with others, work, and God?

Now imagine you have just seen on the big screen a movie based on this perfectly written novel. You have watched the hero, who is you, live through many life experiences and lessons and have been brought through each one wiser, stronger, and more prepared.

You have cheered for her. Laughed and cried with her. You have been her greatest cheerleader.

And now you are sitting in the theatre and wondering what's next for your hero?

Everything has been on purpose to bring you to this new place, this new chapter. You have been groomed for the next adventure. Something bigger and more extraordinary.

You were made to make an impact.

You were created to create.

You were designed for more.

And now it's time to take this novel and move into the next part. Take action.

Dream a little bigger.

Honor the deepest desires of your heart.

Listen to the tiny voice of God whispering, "What's next."

Saturate yourself in love and belief in your worthiness.

As I reflect on this exercise, there are a couple stories that come to mind that I feel compelled to share. It has to do with the chances God gives us to make daily choices to live in love rather than pain. And to write out a happier ending to a difficult story.

One is when my husband left me. Our children were two, three and seven and he'd been home just over a year having spent 12 months overseas in Japan.

He didn't want to be married to me anymore and, shortly after our divorce was final, he was dating another woman and married within a short time.

I was devastated, betrayed, angry and bitter. I wanted him to die.

But in those many times I found myself in pain and crying alone in our former bedroom, I was given an opportunity to rewrite this chapter that was being thrown on me without my agreement or approval.

I could hold onto my feelings of being victimized and share my anger with my children and anyone else who would listen, or I could ask for forgiveness and offer my forgiveness to him.

It was a slow process and there were times I felt justified in being resentful and pitiful. And after many prayers, I continued to seek the higher ground.

I remember one day when my kids asked me what I liked about their dad. I wasn't sure what to say as there wasn't much. But I was determined to find a reasonable and honest answer.

I told them he was passionate about his country. They looked at me with a funny look and I explained he would do anything for the USA as a military man and a retired former Marine to protect our country so we could live in freedom. That seemed to suffice as they never asked me again.

Here's the deal.

I wanted to send an article to the local newspaper of my ex-husband's small town and detail who he really was. But instead, I chose to pray for him and his new wife.

I made the decision not to speak bitter words about him and send out as much love as I could manage each day.

It took 30 years for us to be able to stand in a room together and be civil.

But today, almost 40 years after the finalization of our divorce we are a village. We all love and care for each other, spouses included. We gather as a family when we are celebrating a child or grandchild's birthday.

Forgiveness goes both ways, and I can gratefully say I am a dear friend of his wife, and our families pray for one another when we are going through critical times.

The second story occurred two years after I got married to my current husband, Joseph. I must say I am not sure, even to this point in my life, I have fully grasped what could have happened on that day. I recognized in my head our lives had been spared, but the magnitude of the situation never truly hit me because I couldn't let it. Instead, I just carried on.

Today I wonder, if I could have let it all sink into my heart and soul, would my life be any different in this moment? Would I have lived with more fervor or courage?

FLUID

I don't think so.

I believe we are all where we are supposed to be at any given moment and if it were to be different it would be.

Here's our story.

9/11/2001

My husband and I were to be standing at the top of the World Trade Center at 9:00 a.m. on Sept. 11th, 2001

That's not what happened.

God chose to intercede.

Joe had a Rutger's college reunion scheduled for the weekend of September 15th in New York and we were planning on going a week early to visit his sister who lives across the George Washington bridge in New Jersey.

We love New York and since Joe was born and raised there, we always took every opportunity to go and visit. This was going to be an extra special visit because Joe was taking me to the World Trade Center for the first time. I was excited.

Typically, his sister goes into the city every Tuesday morning for a class and this week we were going to catch a ride with her and go up to the top of the Center while she went to class. She would then pick us up so we could go to lunch and then off to tour the floor of the New York stock exchange.

What a day this was going to be.

But in May, Joe's son Zachary called us with a proposition.

He asked his dad if he'd like free tickets to anywhere in the U.S.

Our ears perked up when Zach said FREE.

His dad asked him what on earth he was talking about.

Zachary worked in a gym in Century City, California and a woman who had been in the gym a few times approached him with the question, "Zach, how would you like free tickets to anywhere in the U.S.?"

He replied that sounded good, but he couldn't take time off work to go anywhere. Could his dad possibly use the tickets instead?

And why did she have free tickets?

She told him she worked for Vanguard Airlines and was authorized to offer free tickets.

Zach called us and asked if we were interested. If so, he would get all the details. It all sounded a bit hokey to us, but what the heck. Seriously, what did we have to lose? He followed up telling us it was totally legitimate, and the only caveat was that we would have to travel before the end of July or lose the tickets.

FREE tickets to New York? No way were we going to lose out on that.

We jumped at the chance. And canceled our September trip.

We traveled in July instead.

So instead of being on the Top of the World Trade Center at 9:00 am on Tuesday 9/11 we were there on a Tuesday morning at 9:00 a.m. on July 10th.

Our lives were spared.

The strange thing is: After getting us the plane tickets, Zachary never saw that woman again, never knew her name, and Vanguard Airlines was bankrupt six months later.

God's timing is always perfect, whether we understand it or not. All we are asked to do is trust Him.

I will never forget this day.

✎ Please turn to your workbooks and dig in.

Three - What baggage did I bring with me from my childhood?

Hm. That's a good question. I know I brought some baggage with me that wasn't true.

The question is, "Who's is it and where did I get it?"

I have been studying the idea that we carry generational ideas and beliefs from farther back than just our parents. What we have brought forward into our daily lives may belong to our ancestors and we don't even know it. We carry it because we were taught it. But not in the traditional way. It's not like we sat down with our parents, and they gave us lessons in controlling our environment, perfectionism, or in being a hyper achiever.

We watched what was going on all around us and soaked up lessons like a dry and parched sponge. We drank in every action and as children we were then left to give meaning to what we saw. Since we cannot live in ambiguity, we must give meaning to what we see and therefore the stories we come up with become our truth and how we live it out, even as adults.

When I was about four years old, the neighbors across the street were having a new room added along with a fireplace. They hired a Spanish speaking laborer to do the brick work and the cementing. Every day he arrived early and brought with him his little boy. I believe his son was about two or three years old.

I must have gone over there a few times and befriended the boy because I remember one day asking my mom if he could come over to our house so he could have lunch and take a nap on my bed.

She said sure and I went and fetched him making sure it was alright with his dad.

He came with me, ate a peanut butter and jelly sandwich and when it was time for him to lay down my mom spread out a towel over my bed.

I had no clue why as she never put a towel there when I laid down. My little four-year-old mind gave it this meaning. His skin color wasn't the same as mine. He was browner and therefore she must have had to protect my bed from someone who was dirty.

There were never any words spoken. Just actions and I have no idea why I thought this was her intentional message. But I carried that with me for many years. People who were a different color must not be as clean as we are. Therefore, they must be dirty and lesser than.

It hurts my heart to even imagine this was the message I took from that experience, but it shows why I am so encouraged to go deeper in my learning. I can't let go of old beliefs if I don't know I have them. And when I can discover where they came from, I can give them back and create my own truth.

My parents raised me in the Catholic faith and sent me to parochial schools all through my growing up years even to private a girls' school on the hill for my high school experience.

I was a curious youngster and asked many questions.

There were numerous times that what I'd been taught in school didn't resonate with my own understanding of Jesus being a kind and loving God.

My parents had a difficult time with me and my questions and told me the way I was being educated was based on the rules of the church. Period.

I eventually stopped asking, accepted what they said as truth and shut my mouth.

But all along I still carried with me conflicting ideas of who God was.

Did He really love me or was He just watching my every move so He could punish me?

It wasn't until many years later when I joined a 12-step program that I began to see that God was a loving father and there wasn't anything I could do to make Him love me anymore or any less then He already did, just the way I am.

I was then able to see the truth for them was not the same truth for me and I could choose how I was going to believe in God according to what felt right for me.

There were other situations where I had to leave behind ideas that no longer resonated with me.

My mom had an interesting relationship with priests.

Somewhere along the way she had developed the idea that all priests were trustworthy and put them on pedestals. Eventually she began to give the same attention and loyalty to any man in power and uniform.

I learned these ways of believing which often caught me off guard and put me in a place of being abused.

I believed and trusted in those who hadn't earned my trust.

And slowly I could see that just because she believed that way didn't mean I had to.

As I continued to grow up and even to today, I must pause and pray before I believe everything that's out before me.

I am responsible for what I believe, which feeds how I make choices. With each choice made comes a consequence that not only affects me but others as well.

✎ Look at the questions in your workbook and continue your journey.

Four - What ideas no longer feel in alignment with who I am and want to become?

There is so much we've covered up to this point that suggests we are who we are today based on many factors. Lessons we were taught, ideas we've held, what society tells us about who we should be and the definitions and truths we've given to our life's experiences.

Since we are always learning and growing there comes a time on our journey when we are jolted into the notion that maybe who we are isn't who we want to be. Maybe it's time to shed old thought patterns to make room for new ones. Maybe we have reached a point where we are sick and tired of being sick and tired.

How many times were we told we weren't smart enough, pretty enough, thin enough, good enough, whatever enough to do what we most wanted to do?

How many times were we shown that how we completed a task or did a chore needed to be redone by someone who could do it better?

And we walked away, yet again, reinforcing in our own minds we could never do anything right.

Those are the ideas from a long time ago, but they still show up as truth today.

Why is that?

Why are our automatic thoughts so negative?

Why have we allowed other's opinions of who we should be matter so much?

I think it all goes back to our conditioning.

If we grew up with little money, then often we believe we will never have enough money.

If we never felt loved as a child, then we grow up believing we are not worthy of love.

If everyone was always in a hurry in our households, we might carry the message that there's never enough time.

And if we lived in a chaotic home with mixed messages, we find ourselves in similar situations as adults because that's what we knew. It's uncomfortably comfortable.

As I go back through the chapters of my life, I can see the common thread was my fear of abandonment and rejection. No one ever left me physically but there was no one there to care for my emotional needs. I never felt seen or heard.

I asked too many questions and was labeled as "TOO." I was too smart. Too inquisitive. Too emotional. Too intense. Too sensitive. Too needy. Too talkative. TOO……whatever.

And I carried that truth with me.

Since being abandoned lived so deeply within me each decision I made was prompted by that fear.

I could never say no because if I did you might never ask me to do anything with you again. I couldn't set boundaries because if I made you angry you would walk away. If I didn't want to marry you but just wanted to be with you, something bad might happen because I was living in sin with a man I wasn't married to.

Therefore, I continued to say yes when all I really wanted to do was say no.

When I was 7 months pregnant my husband said he wanted to move from Costa Mesa and buy a house in Riverside. I had just debuted as a new Mary Kay Sales director and all my clients and team members were in Costa Mesa. My family and support system lived locally as well and now I was leaving it all behind to move to the desert with a four-year-old and a baby on the way.

I was nearly to term when we finally closed on the house and as I was putting pots and pans into our new kitchen, I went into labor and had to drive back to Newport Beach where I had my daughter, Katie, the next day at Hoag Hospital.

It wasn't too long after Katie was born that I was pregnant with Shawn and when he was two my husband made the ultimate decision he didn't want to be married anymore and left.

With three children under the age of seven I clung to my friend across the street for support until the day she said, "Who will ever want to marry you with three kids?"

There it was.

Who will ever want you?

So, when I met a man who was tattooed from head to toe, and he suggested we go out for a date I said yes even though I wasn't sure that was what I wanted. And nine months later I married him.

Was I positive I was in love with him? No. But I was sure I didn't want to be alone, so I said yes. If I had taken more time, I may have understood my motives and chosen to walk away instead.

My underlying fear colored every choice I made from my friends to my 43-year career, to the home I live in. Once I was all in, there was no going back.

The idea that I had a voice but was not allowed to use it followed me all the way into my first, second and third marriage.

It wasn't until I began my journey into coaching that I began to see how desperate I was to tell my truth.

Even with years of therapy, I didn't uncover some of these vital truths until I started working with my own personal coach.

✎ What in this chapter resonates with you? In your workbook make a note of what you're learning and how it can change your life.

Five - Do you feel safe in your world today?

I'm not sure why I asked this question other than I felt led to do so. I wondered what it might mean to others and realized I needed to ask myself first.

What does safe mean?

Protected from or not exposed to danger or risk, not likely to be harmed or lost.

In the past I never felt safe in my world. I was always suspicious of people's motives and agendas. My mom and dad were unpredictable, and I thought that all adults were not to be trusted. They say one thing and do another.

The problem with this mindset was that I was looking for reasons to not trust others. I was vigilant in my observation of people around me, constantly wondering if they could be counted on.

My mantra was, "Never mind. I'll do it myself." Because if I just did life alone, I wouldn't be hurt from promises made and unfulfilled by others. Along my path many people proved through their behavior to be responsible and trustworthy. However, the lenses I saw life through were covered with skepticism.

Who I observed people to be was different after I gave them my trust. I was hurt so I soon learned that all are guilty of something until proven innocent.

The question I now ask myself is more about emotional pain, and am I equipped enough to recognize when I am being harmed by someone else's words and/or actions?

I have been married for 25 years to a man who is 21 years my senior and his world is shrinking. He cannot see due to macular degeneration and can't walk without a walker. His driving privileges have been taken away and he can no longer play golf.

He is often angry and frustrated and takes these feelings out on me.

Do I feel safe in my home living with him? Not always. When I am tired and have little energy to set my personal boundaries it can be difficult to hold my tongue. Do I leave him because he is accusatory and now doesn't trust me? I have thought about it. I have thought a lot about it, but I am not ready to make that decision. I married him with the intention to live out my vows as honestly and truly as I can.

But let's be clear. Is it easy? Oh, definitely not. I must decide each day to be married. I don't look into the future to figure out what I should do next week, next month or next year. I take it one day at a time.

And it's only doable when I make sure my cup is filled and I am not running on empty.

It is necessary and vital that I take self-care seriously. To be quiet long enough to check in with my body, mind and spirit and see what I am lacking or when I need to refuel my emotional gas tank.

When I take care of me it's easier to take care of him and step away when his actions are not acceptable or tolerable.

I know what he does and says is not personal. His behavior belongs to him. If I choose not to react but simply walk out of the room, it keeps me from running away from home.

I believe I am strong enough to set the appropriate boundaries to keep my heart protected but only when I am present in the moment and mindful of what's happening in front of me.

Today I know what that pain feels like and can recognize it when it's happening.

Truth be told, it is always more about me than about anyone else. My humanness wants to blame others for my reactionary behaviors. My first thought is how can I defend myself against anyone making derogatory remarks about me. And especially if I am being accused of something I haven't done.

But lately I have been learning that when I am accused, it's best that I just be quiet. It is not necessary to prove who I am to anyone.

I know who I am and that should be enough.

But when I am unsure of how I am feeling in my own skin, it puts my mind in a precarious place and my thinking becomes distorted, I lose sight of how God sees me and I begin to feel the need to attack others on my own behalf.

Recently after an appointment with a couple's counselor I made the decision to each day put on my love glasses and start seeing my husband the way I saw him years ago when we fell in love.

I tell him each morning three things I see in him that I admire.

I recognized how in the past few months my focus has been on the things he's been doing that hurt me and then continuing to feed my pain by ruminating on the possibility he's been doing this on purpose to cause me pain.

I know better. I understand the victim's mindset. It has been something I have worked on for a long time and yet, even after all my training, learning and constant prayers, I can still so easily fall back into that old place.

I believe it might be something I get to deal with forever, but as I continue to wake up, emotionally and spiritually I get better.

I'm not perfect, but I find myself moving more quickly out of toxic thinking and behaving more quickly.

I remember years ago when I was visiting Florida for a Mary Kay leadership conference and met up with a woman I had become friends with through my second's husband's racing days. She was the mom of a drag racer in the 1980's. I had called her while I was in town and asked if I could offer a free facial from my hotel room looking over Biscayne Bay. She gladly agreed and on a sunny afternoon we had the chance to catch up and talk while I shared the Mary Kay experience with her.

As I looked out of the hotel room over the bay I said aloud, "How can someone look out at this view and not believe in God?"

And she said, "It's not what you're looking at. It's what you're looking with."

I have never forgotten the words she spoke that day and have carried them with me since then.

So now I am reminded when I am frustrated with another's behavior or attitude to take a closer look at me rather than them. I will most likely find my answer as to why I am so bothered by my fellow human being.

✎ Workbook time again.

FLUID

CHAPTER 4

Intuition: what's been calling me?

One - Are you an overthinker or over feeler?

I always thought I was more of a feeler than a thinker.

But as I continue my journey to wholeness, I can see that although I am a deep feeling woman, I have used my mind to keep me safe.

I have perfected the art of over analyzing every word and action of others. I have moved into over thinking when my heart couldn't take the pain anymore.

The pain of rejection, abandonment, loss.

Often enough it was my own interpretation of the events around me that caused my heartache more than the actions of others.

But moving from my head to my heart would cause me to really see what was going on. If I wasn't ready to deal with the truth, I just stayed in a place that kept my eyes shadowed and my soul in the fog.

I didn't want to see that maybe the problem all along was more about how I labeled others than what was true. Over thinking was how I escaped, and it served me well until it didn't.

Doing some research, I learned about over thinkers from Houston Methodist.

Signs that you might be overthinking include:

- Dwelling on past events or situations.
- Second-guessing decisions you've made.
- Replaying your mistakes in your mind.

- Rehashing challenging or uncomfortable conversations.
- Fixating on things you can't control, change, or improve.
- Imagining the worst-case scenario or outcome.
- Following your worries out of the present moment and into an unchangeable past or unforeseeable future.
- "Running your list" while trying to fall asleep.
- Questioning but never deciding or taking action.

You can get caught in the idea that you are simply problem solving but there is a difference. Problem solving is when you ask questions with the intent of finding an answer or enacting a solution. Overthinking is when you perseverate on possibilities and pitfalls without any real intent of solving anything. It sounds more like one is living out being a victim rather than figuring out how to be victorious.

You may be wondering what this has to do with intuition. I believe when we get caught in our heads it makes it harder to hear that small voice inside that's giving us wise direction on the next step we need to take in our lives.

However, over feeling can keep us stuck in an emotional place. This can create difficulty in combining thinking with feeling to navigate our lives in healthy patterns of living.

My dad was an overthinker. He was a great navigator when it came to details and directions outside of himself.

He used his ability to think more with positive intentions rather than dwelling on situations he couldn't control. I grew up believing that thinking was great and that's all one needed to understand how to live a normal, healthy life.

Every year he took a group of people to explore the bottom of the Grand Canyon and I would watch him in awe as he went about the intricate details of putting this trip together. He had numerous typewritten lists of food, planned menus, necessary equipment, hotel reservations needed along the way, name, and numbers for emergencies.

The garage floor was covered with a tarp so he could place everything in an orderly position before he packed up making absolutely sure all was in perfect order.

He never missed a detail and as he went along, he would check off each thing on his list and then he'd double check before he left.

He was like this in many areas of his life. Control was his main pattern along with perfectionistic tendencies. My dad was amazing in that way.

Methodical, organized and very systemized.

Great when it came to camping but not so good when it came to parenting.

I got my creativity from my dad, but his methodical brain clearly passed me by.

I recall when my grandmother, his mom, had a stroke. He received word by phone from my aunt as my grandma lived in North Carolina and we lived in California. I was married by then and living in Riverside, my parents lived in Costa Mesa. My grandfather had already died so she was his only living parent.

Dad had come to Riverside to help with something I needed and as he was leaving, I followed him out to the car. I stood there next to him and asked, "What does it feel like to have your only living parent getting ready to die?" I couldn't imagine what that would feel like if it were happening to me.

His answer was, "It feels like I'm going to have to go to a funeral."

I knew then my dad wouldn't know a feeling if it jumped up and bit him in the fanny.

His inability to express any feelings caused problems for not only him and my mom but for all of us as a family.

I'm not sure if it was a man thing not to engage in feelings because in his generation it was not encouraged. Or if he was born with the mind of an engineer and didn't really know how to explore the part of him that carried his ability to feel. I'm not sure I can't recall a time when I saw him cry.

I used to believe he didn't know how to feel but I believe everyone has feelings and maybe they just don't know how to label them and/or express them.

I know our lives would have been so much richer if we could have had honest conversations around what brought us the greatest amount of pain and joy. It would have opened the doors to really knowing one another and thus loving each member of our family in a deeper way.

Using your mind to reason things out is truly a gift but when our gifts are thrown to the extreme, they create havoc in our lives and relationships.

Over feeler: the definition of an over feeler is so simple. One who feels excessively or to too great an extent.

DUH!!!!

I can't say whether we are born as an overthinker or feeler, but I can say our childhood upbringing can influence what we use to feel safer in our environment.

I tend more to the feeling side than the thinking side.

I was emotional. I internalized life in my gut. As a child I asked a ton of questions when things didn't "feel right" on the inside.

My head would tell me one thing, but my intuition would say otherwise.

When you're little and something feels off in your home you really can't say that you know something is wrong because families tend to hide what might really be going on. They don't want the kids to be alarmed or afraid, so they stay silent and keep the secret hidden.

If parents are thinking of divorce the thinkers may see that everything seems normal. They are still talking, sleeping in the same bed, and doing what they have always done.

The feelers tend to go inward and begin to intuit what isn't being said into an idea that there is a problem, and they must put a name on it so they can live with what they are feeling. Uncertainty and confusion. Children have a challenging time living with mixed messages so they create a story in their minds they can live with. It may not be true but at least they can sleep at night, at least for the moment.

From Psychology Today: Feeling intensely: The Wounds of Being "Too Much."

People who feel more deeply and intensely than others are more aware of subtleties; their brain processes information and reflects on it more deeply. People with emotional intensity are sometimes described as sensitive, caring, and attentive. At their best, they can be exceptionally perceptive, intuitive, and keenly observant of the subtleties of <u>the environment</u>. Yet they are also overwhelmed by the constant waves of social nuances and others' emotional and psychic energies. –

They tend to notice and remember a lot and can be overstimulated when things are too chaotic or novel for a long time. This ability to feel deeply and intensely often starts from a young age when <u>emotion regulation</u> skills are lacking and can lead to psychological wounding associated with <u>shame</u> and <u>loneliness</u>.

Growing awareness of this trait has generated much inquiry, yet psychologists have so far been unable to agree on a single defining attribute. If you identify with the description, there are a few possibilities:

- *This may mean that you are one of the 15-20 percent of the population wired differently as a <u>Highly Sensitive Person</u>.*

- *This may mean that you fall on the right side of the bell curve as a gifted person.*

- *This may mean you have or are mislabeled as having a mental illness such as Emotion Regulation Disorder, <u>ADHD</u>, <u>Bipolar Disorder</u>, or Dysthymia (chronic <u>depression</u>).*

The world is gradually coming to embrace the concept of <u>neurodiversity</u> — the idea that particular groups of the population are «different» from the norm, with specific kinds of sensitivity, intensity, and <u>giftedness</u>. However, with little awareness, many emotionally intense adults confessed to having felt lonely and misunderstood for years, being plagued with self-doubts, and living with a lingering sense of existential loneliness.

End of article-

I was one of those kids who grew up feeling like I never fit in. I thought there might be something wrong with me that I didn't easily warm up to other kids in my class. I was distant, more of an observer rather than a participant.

Could it be because of a crazy home life I needed to keep secret from others? I can't remember ever having friends over for a sleep over.

I know everyone loved my dad because he took care of the neighborhood. He delivered a baby of the woman across the street before the paramedics arrived. He fixed all the kids' broken bicycles. We had the best-looking house each holiday adorned with every handmade decoration you could think of. But what happened behind our doors was never spoken about to the neighbors. We were good at pretending to be what we weren't.

Maybe because I was such a deep feeling child, I sensed things more. Even today when I ask my siblings questions about growing up, they don't see many of our experiences like I do. I often wondered how I came from my own family. I didn't feel like I fit in there either and thus went forward in my life carrying those same feelings.

I have always been quite curious and still am, often bugging family and friends with a gazillion questions, and wondering if this was learned or was I born this way.

Does it really matter? Do I have to know why? Or can I accept this is who I am today and leave it at that?

When I ask the question "why," it's generally my need to control life. If I know why then I can fix it, change it, make it better. Maybe it's totally okay not to change it. To let it be. To let ME be. To let others be.

Today I am more comfortable in my own skin. I don't have the same need to have answers. I can let life be without trying to control outside circumstances and results. I am always in a state of evolving to be a better version of myself. I don't want to be stagnant, so I am continually seeking to grow.

If I was born this way or became curious out of a need to control the cards I was dealt is it possible to find ways to make these skills a gift rather than finding fault in how I navigate life?

I believe acceptance of who I am today gives me more freedom to live a fulfilling life while letting go of others' opinions, constant internal criticism and thinking I am less than because I am not like you.

Just because I don't feel like I fit doesn't mean I don't belong.

Over thinker? Over feeler? Who cares?

If you're satisfied with being who you are then that's all that matters. And if you're not it just means you have more growing to do.

✎ Bring out the workbook and see if some of the questions can reveal where there might be work needed for your ongoing transformation.

Two - Do you give yourself time each day to be still and listen to your intuitive voice?

There were so many times in my life when I was too overwhelmed and exhausted to even think about giving myself a time out for quiet reflection. There was no use even considering it because my plate was overflowing with responsibilities, and I had barely enough time to take a shower. I gave up on me so I could care for everyone else.

These behavior patterns served me well, or at least that's what I told myself until I almost had a nervous breakdown.

Prior to thinking a nervous breakdown could ever be in my future, I was building a Mary Kay business while being married to a man who was a recovering alcoholic. He had attended school at night to be a drug and alcohol counselor for the military and on the weekdays, he left before dawn and got home after the sun went down. The kids rarely saw him, and I felt like a married single.

After we moved to Riverside and we had our third child, my husband was sent orders to serve a year overseas in Japan. I was a nervous wreck thinking about it and by the time he actually got on the plane the children were three months, 21 months and five years old. The five-year-old had been hit by a car before his dad left and was in a full leg cast using crutches to get himself in and out of his kindergarten class.

How in heaven's name was I going to get through this next year trying to run a business and care for such a young family? The only way I could was to not think about it and take the next indicated step.

We all managed, but when he got home life here had changed. And I had changed. I had become quite independent and a year later he decided he wanted a divorce.

Our marriage lasted for ten years, and the divorce was finalized on our youngest son's second birthday.

What now?

I picked myself up by the bootstraps and kept going.

That was how I did life. Picking up the broken pieces and moving on.

During my second marriage my ex-husband took another overseas tour to Japan taking with him the woman he married after he left me.

As my oldest son, now 14, struggled with my marriage to his stepdad he decided he wanted to go visit his dad overseas. I was exhausted from standing in between an angry teenager and a frustrated husband so I let my son go stay for six weeks.

But when he called after two weeks and said he wanted to remain in Japan, my heart was broken.

As tired as I was with the situation, I was not prepared to let him go and I started to slip into a deep depression.

He stayed with his dad for two years coming home for one visit before he returned to the states permanently.

I was so overwhelmed by my sense of unfelt and undealt with loss I could barely function.

I cried often. I was distracted, confused, and felt lost in the dark.

If my intuition had used a blow horn to get my attention, I couldn't have heard it. The little voice trying to find its way to my head was covered too deeply by my sorrow and sadness. It was there but there was no way I could find it.

And frankly I didn't even know I needed it.

I prayed at night laying near the fireplace with my head on my Bible. I took bubble baths that lasted so long the water grew ice cold. I was silent.

I finally went to my doctor and told him I needed a mammogram. He told me I was only 34 with no history of cancer in my family and was concerned by my desperate need to have the test done.

However, we had a history together and he knew me and how I functioned. After a lengthy conversation he recognized the deep fear I was carrying around about getting sick. He told me he didn't think I had cancer but that he would order the tests to ease my mind.

He said he believed the pain was coming from a broken heart. I knew he was right when the test results came back negative.

There were moments during this time I thought I was headed to the hospital for a 51/50. I was scared. I was engulfed with feelings so strong I had trouble coming up for air. But through the continued guidance of a good primary care doctor, I got the help I needed and came through the dark with a renewed sense of survival and confidence.

The story of my life really didn't ease up much, but I was more aware and mindful of pitfalls that could trigger my fear of feeling unsafe and unable to cope with life. I put my second husband in jail for attempted manufacturing of meth in the garage and served him divorce papers while he was there.

My youngest son chose to go live with his dad in Washington when he was 16. This time was easier.

All three kids struggled with drug addiction and alcoholism at the same time.

And I married again this time to a man who is 21 years my senior.

Today I live as his caregiver. And have retired as a Mary Kay Sales Director after holding the position for 41 years.

I could use the same excuse I've always used to not allow myself time to stop, listen and be still. To allow space in my daily routine to hear the voice of the Holy Spirit guiding me to my next step. I could pull myself up by the bootstraps and keep going.

Today I know better. What I believed served me when I was younger was the lie that I could do everything I needed without help. I was the SUPERWOMAN of the family. I was the hero and believed it.

Those beliefs almost cost me my sanity and my emotional and physical health.

There was no harmony is my daily life and we all suffered for it.

Oh, I earned Pink Cadillacs, numerous diamond rings and titles, but those never filled the hole in my soul that only God could fill, and how would He ever be able to do that if I refused to stop long enough to admit to myself and Him that I needed guidance and help to answer His call?

For the last couple years, I have known in my gut it was time to let go of the Mary Kay leadership role. But I wasn't ready. I had spent more than two thirds of my life in this career and although I had been training to be a life coach, I wasn't emotionally capable of releasing the dream I held so tight to. I knew it was time. I didn't want it to be time. I wanted to hold on. I wanted to do both Mary Kay and coaching, but my heart was being pulled from one arena to another and I knew. It wasn't until this year that I truly surrendered to what my intuition had been telling me all along.

So, on my 41-year anniversary I stepped away from my Mary Kay business and began to coach full time. I am still a beauty consultant but no longer lead people to their dreams in the business.

Was it an easy choice? Absolutely not.

Was I terrified? You bet I was.

The cost felt so high. But I knew it was the right choice.

Just because I listened to the small voice showing me my next step, it still wasn't easy.

I couldn't believe He was asking me to let this go. I had dreams here. I thought I'd be here forever. My humanness wanted to argue. I wanted more signs I was doing the right thing. I wanted God to write me a handwritten gold letter telling me this was IT!

I wanted guarantees.

The only guarantee I get and continue to receive is the one where He tells me He loves me. He will guide me in the direction He wants me to go, and He will be with me on my journey.

And that's enough for me.

What about you?

✎ Turn to your workbooks and see what you discover.

Three - What's your inner self calling you to do?

For the longest time I didn't know I had an inner self because the noise outside me caused so much chaos I couldn't hear that voice trying to tell me something new. I don't think it was because I was denying the voice of God which for me is where that voice comes from. I was just too caught up in my everyday life of growing up, having a family, working a business, and trying to stay married.

Trusting my intuition would mean I needed to take a slow break during the day to quiet my mind and listen, but I was too busy.

I became more curious about what my intuition was saying.

I was the president of my local Kiwanis Club, and we were at a board meeting early one Tuesday morning at Panera Bread. As I sat there to address our board members, I kept hearing that little voice telling me to buy a loaf of bread for Gayle.

Gayle was a Mary Kay customer and friend who had recently lost her dad. I was grateful to have met him when I brought him an angel blanket. She called a few days prior to tell me because she thought I would like to know. I was.

But when the voice began speaking to me in the middle of my meeting, I thought I was going to lose my mind.

Trying to stay focused while having an ongoing inner dialogue with the Holy Spirit was hysterical. It was funny to me because no one knew what I was doing in my head at the time.

This is how it went:

H.S. Buy Gayle a loaf of bread.

Me: What? Are you kidding me? I'm in the middle of a meeting.

H. S. I know. Buy her a loaf of bread after your meeting.

Me: What? Buy Gayle a loaf of bread and do what with it? Leave it on her door?

H.S. Exactly.

Me: So, you want me to buy a loaf of bread, put it in a Mary Kay bag and leave it on her door? Do I get her a card too?

H.S. Yep.

Me: Really? This sounds ridiculous. She is going to think I have lost my marbles.

H.S. What does it matter that she thinks. I WANT you to buy her a loaf of bread.

After I adjourned the meeting and finished my coffee guess what I did?

You got it. I bought a loaf of bread, went to Von's and got a sympathy card and drove to Gayle's to leave it on her door.

I snuck away praying no one saw me to ask what I was doing in her front yard.

After a couple days I got a call and saw it was Gayle. I hesitated for only a minute thinking she was going to ask me what drove me out of my mind.

Quite the opposite. She thanked me. Friends had brought them dinner and a salad that Tuesday night, but no one had brought the bread and it was the bread I bought they used to break and share in honor of her dad. I was in absolute awe of how God used me to bless her, but it was such a quiet message that I could have missed the whole experience.

I had a choice that morning. I could follow His lead and be obedient or I could simply shush it and go about doing what my next step was that day.

My ego could have hijacked me and said I would look ridiculous, and she would think I was nuts.

In the end I choose to listen and follow God. And we were all grateful.

Not too many years later I kept having dreams of painting. Not houses but pictures. I loved to draw as a kid but never had any inclination towards painting. The dreams continued and I knew it was a message I was supposed to explore.

Dreams have a way of communicating things I cannot seem to hear during the day.

My first thought was, "Now that's interesting. Paint? Me? No way. No time."

I put the idea away and went on with my life.

A year or so later Mary Kay was offering a complete artist set as a prize for Star Consultants. It had everything one would need other than the paper and brushes. Watercolors, acrylics, colored pencils, chalk, and you could use the box as a tabletop easel.

There it was. No more excuses. And I set it aside for a full year and never opened the box.

It wasn't until my husband Joe and I decided to pack our little Honda Civic and drive across country for a trip of a lifetime that I decided it was time. Joe asked, "This is the time for what?"

I responded, "For me to bring my paint set."

"You want to bring the paint set in the car with us along with everything else we are taking"?

"Yep."

And so, it was.

The artist set found its way into the back seat, and I took it to 35 states and over 10,000 miles delightfully painting along the way.

The first painting I did was in Great Barrington, MA overlooking 30 acres of farmland and I was hooked.

I used watercolors because I was afraid Joe might have a reaction to acrylics since he had lung issues.

Come to find out these new acrylics don't have much smell and it would have been fine.

I have been painting ever since and even had an art show the year following our trip.

The hardest part of picking up the paint brush was the fear that I would suck at it. And my childhood memories were of family saying that hobbies just cost you money and if you can't sell what you make then don't waste your time or resources.

I made the decision to go where my dreams were taking me and I am so glad I did.

Today even if I am not perfect at what I'm doing I've decided if the activity brings me joy then I am going to do it no matter what anyone else says.

And then there are those other times when I choose not to listen to that voice and reap the consequences. Like when I was 18 and went snow skiing with friends. I didn't know how to ski but didn't want to miss out or be left behind, so I went anyway. I started out on the little hill and after some practice I was encouraged to go higher by my then boyfriend.

I knew it wasn't a good idea. My intuition was telling me to be done, but I had something to prove or so I thought.

I went higher and came crashing down. I ended up in the silver cart being carried down the mountain by the ski patrol. Off to the ER with a twisted and sprained knee and on crutches for six weeks.

It's the same knee I had replaced five years ago.

Was that because of my accident? I don't think I'll ever know. But what I do know is if I had listened and acted upon my intuition, I would never have had the accident in the first place.

It's in those tranquil moments of solitude I hear the whisper.

For a long time, I wouldn't listen because I associated God's voice with the voice of my earthly father, and he was abusive and couldn't be trusted.

I was afraid God would ask me to do something that was impossible or to let go of something I cherished. I was always waiting for the next shoe to drop or for the punishment of not getting something right enough. I was skeptical of God's love.

I ran away from Him because I was too afraid to run towards Him.

I look back and wonder what was I trying to prove? Who was I trying to impress and was it worth silencing that quiet whisper? Was I so fearful of being harmed that I couldn't see the true love God had for me, His perfectly imperfect child?

As I grew, I could see that nothing is worth silencing His voice. It was all a learning lesson and continues to be. I wish I could say that all I needed was to pay closer attention but that's not the case.

Slow learner, I guess. It took many more opportunities and a lot of grace and patience.

Today I can appreciate that each of us has our own personal learning curve, our own way of processing life's experiences, our own way of understanding. And God's timing is perfect. We need not try to hurry God along or feel guilty that we are not further in our progress.

There are no mistakes and everything that happens is done for us and not TO us. It's all about embracing the journey as it has been designed with less resistance and more acceptance, one step and one day at a time.

✏ Please open your workbooks and continue.

Four - How do you feel and what do you do when you hear that small voice speaking?

The inner noise that bombarded me from the past was too loud, not to mention all the information being thrown at me on a daily basis from sources too many to count.

Rarely did I give myself time to sit and quiet my spirit.

There was too much that needed my attention.

Work, children, husbands who were coming and going. The daily chaos that comes from living with alcoholism and addiction and all the ripple effects that come with that.

If I am really going to be honest, I think I was afraid of that voice. It was easier to stay busy than to stop and listen. What if I was being asked to do something I didn't feel confident doing?

What if I knew it was time to make a change and I didn't have the courage to follow through?

I was so filled with fear of the unknown that I would stop myself in my tracks before I would listen to anything God was trying to say. I would immediately put my hands over my ears and start with the" LaLa" mantra so I couldn't hear His message. There had been so many times in my past when I did what those in charge of my life told me to do and was harmed in the process. I could sense I was willing to surrender 95% of my life to God but would adamantly hold on to the last 5 % in case the other shoe came flying at my head. I knew in my head that wasn't the case but, in my heart, I carried a different belief. I wanted to listen and obey. I was just too frightened to allow myself that freedom.

Today life is so different.

I have come to a new understanding of how God loves me and protects me from things I am not ready for.

He is gracious and kind in His timing. As I have grown as a woman, I have grown in my relationship with Him. I am learning to trust with greater ease. I am surrendering without fighting so hard to run my own life. I am granting myself permission to be quiet and rest.

It is in the development of that trust I find myself seeking more space to listen and learn.

As I go the riverbank in my mind to sit with Jesus and pour out my heart, I feel safe to tell Him everything. It's a place of comfort and I share whatever is on my mind. I know there is no judgment, only love and during those times with Him it feels like I am a child who is having an open and honest conversation with my daddy.

I never had an earthly dad I could talk to, so this is a new experience for me.

The process of trusting is no easy task when you have been beaten up by those you believed loved you and were supposed to have your best interest at heart. There is no blame today for what my parents couldn't give or do while I was growing up. They did the best they could and although I wish it could have been better, I am grateful for what they could give. I have forgiven them for what they couldn't do. I know there may come a time in my life when my children will have to come to the same conclusions about me and how I parented them. Am I ready for that day? I hope so, but only time will tell.

After I retired from my business there was much more time to ponder where I have been and where I want to go. In those moments I can continually hear God's sweet whisper, "I've got you. I have everything all figured out. You can rest for a while. Listen to the birds sing. Watch the sunsets. Read for a while. Sit at my feet and be a Mary. Let go of what you thought you needed and relax in knowing that I am your source."

My greatest challenge today is not hearing the voice but honoring the voice. Being obedient to God's suggestions when they don't make sense to me. Trusting He has a plan and it's ok not to be always working, seeking other's approval and being productive.

The lessons from childhood were about idle hands being the devil's workshop. The harder you worked, the more you achieved. If you took time off everything you had worked for would be taken away and lost. No rest for the weary. Don't give up. Keep going.

But at what cost? What have we sacrificed and lost to gain so much? Broken marriages traded in for a bigger bank account? Wounded and emotionally abandoned children for the sake of a more beautiful car?

I am no longer feeling bound to what society tells me I should or should not be doing.

I am no longer finding myself seeking other's approval or validation.

I am no longer willing to betray myself so you can be comfortable.

How is this possible?

Only through the grace of God and doing my part as I seek God's will in my everyday life.

✎ Get out your workbook and take a look at the new questions.

Five - When something doesn't feel right do you feel it and honor it? If not, why not?

There have been more times than I can count when I stuffed that intuitive voice down into the deepest, darkest place of my mind. I couldn't listen to it because I was too afraid of what would happen next if I did.

What if the message was to let go of something I wanted so desperately?

What if I was being asked to step into something that was way too big for me to understand?

If something didn't feel right, what would transpire if I used my voice and spoke up? Would my world, as I knew it, fall apart leaving me emotionally naked and vulnerable to the world?

All I know today is that when we are not ready to listen, it's because the fear is bigger than we are. But it won't always be that way.

There will come a time when not recognizing that small voice inside will end up coming out as a roar in the most unusual places. It will be directed at an innocent bystander who doesn't deserve your anger. It might pop up in a conversation with your spouse or your children and you will wonder where that energy came from. It might even surprise you.

When we don't honor our intuition, it doesn't go away. It continues to speak to us quietly until the only way it can grab our attention is through an outburst of some kind.

Sometimes it comes through an illness. When we are in a place of dis-ease in our bodies the energy has no place to go other than create a situation that will demand our attention.

Maybe it's only when a relationship breaks, and we are standing in the dark with the pieces of our marriage broken and at our feet.

These 'knowings' can't become unknowings just because we refuse to listen and honor what they are saying.

There will be a time when we will be forced to turn towards the messages and hear what they have been trying to teach us all along.

When I was married to my second husband, I was told by a friend that someone in my home was using drugs, and I knew who it was.

I had suspected it was my husband but was so caught up in my denial I basically turned my head away and refused to honor what I knew. The truth is if I admitted to knowing I would then have to take responsibility to change it. And that would require more courage than I thought I had at the time.

So, I ignored it until I couldn't pretend anymore.

My oldest son had known for two years my husband was using because he had found drug paraphernalia under the bathroom sink. But he kept it a secret to protect me from having to make any decisions he knew I wasn't ready to make. He didn't want to be the one to break my denial and cause my heart to break. So, I was granted two extra years to live in my own darkness while being provided a way to, yet again, avoid the inevitable.

As I look back it makes me sad to think he carried that with him for so long not wanting me to be hurt any more than I already had been, married to his stepdad. It was not his place to be my protector, but he understood how fragile I felt from watching our day-to-day actions with one another.

Finally, he came to me and told me everything he knew. He and his brother and sister opened a carry bag and took out every bit of drug stuff, poured it out on the table and asked me to do something.

I had no clue what I was looking at and felt helpless on what my next step was. I was shocked but not surprised. My denial had finally been stripped away and I was left holding on to broken light bulbs, razor blades, tin foil, and drinking straws. I put it all in a large Mary Kay bag and dropped it in my purse until I could figure out what my plan of action was.

It wasn't but a couple days later I confided in a friend about what the kids had found. She stood there looking at me and then said, "You need to go to the police right away."

I swallowed hard and replied, "There is no way I am going to the cops. There must be another way to deal with this."

She reminded me her husband was an attorney and his experience was if the police had any inkling my husband was involved with drugs they could come, search my home, confiscate any paraphernalia they found and put me in jail with him. And then take my kids and place them in protective foster care until I could prove my innocence.

As we talked about the possible nightmare unfolding, it scared me to death, and I agreed to go to the police and give them all that I had.

I told my husband I was going out for a cup of coffee with my girlfriend, and she drove me downtown to the police headquarters. When we arrived, it was a little after 5:00 p.m. and the doors to the main office were closed. I was relieved and told her it must be a sign to forget it and just go home. She was adamant about not giving me an out and told me so. We stood around the back of the station for a few minutes. As I begged her to drive me home with a promise I would go back later in the week the back door opened and out walked three uniformed police officers.

She walked right up to them and asked for their help.

I poured the contents of the bag onto the hood of their car and with a curious look they asked where I got all this stuff. I told them it belonged to my husband, and they requested I allow them to follow me home to question him.

I was horrified and told them that was not possible because he was at home with my kids, and I wasn't sure how he would react when they got there.

They understood completely and assured me I would be okay.

In that split second, I realized that protecting my children and myself was far more important than keeping the secrets of an active addict and I was willing to face the truth no matter what the end results were.

The police drove up right behind me, came into the house, took my husband into the garage, hand-cuffed him and began to search the premises.

I felt sick to my stomach.

With the garage door open and the neighbors coming out of the woodwork, the process had begun. The kids were angry even though they were the ones who asked me to do something. I think they were shocked I had actually stepped up since I had shown them prior, I wasn't very brave. As they screamed at me, my friend took me by the arm and led me inside. She knew I didn't need to watch the police and feel the rage of my children all at the same time. I appreciated her doing for me what I couldn't since I felt frozen in my tracks not knowing what to do next.

My husband was arrested.

And when we all caught our breath, the kids began searching places the police hadn't thought to look.

Pornography on the computer.

Empty Drixoral tablets stuffed in the lining of the dog food bag.

Eye droppers inside the gas tank of the motorcycle he had purchased behind my back.

I was in shock.

The indications were far beyond my understanding. My spouse was trying to manufacture meth in our garage.

How could I have missed so many signs pointing in the direction of disaster? Was I that blind or stupid?

I was neither. Not only was I uneducated but I was in denial.

I had lived with drinkers before but never had I experienced such secrecy and deceit. I was embarrassed for not knowing. But when you don't, won't or can't hear that voice telling you something is wrong, it will often take a crisis to bring your head out of the sand.

I had hit the wall. My children had hit the wall. There was nothing more I could do to pretend my life was good. It wasn't good and now the truth was staring me in the face.

I was incredibly grateful no one had been hurt and our home hadn't blown up.

My husband was arrested for attempted manufacturing of meth and put in jail.

It took a bit of time for me to process the gravity of my situation, but with friends who could see what I couldn't I made the decision to serve him divorce papers while he was incarcerated.

He was released from jail 30 days later. I didn't ask any particulars on how that all played out for him since I was focused on moving forward with my life and the lives of the kids.

Today, many years later, I can tell you my ex has made amends to me and my children. I have made my amends as well. We have both remarried and accepted Jesus as his savior and is living a life of freedom, both physically and spiritually.

God is good even when our worlds seem to be falling apart.

✎ Open your workbooks and promise yourself you will answer your questions as honestly and authentically as possible.

Six - Is it wise to trust what you know?

I always thought it was wise to trust what I know, but as I sat down to write this today, I wondered if doing that was really a good thing.

There are truths that will always be pertinent for me. I will forever believe God loves me. Jesus died for my sins, and I am forgiven. These truths are nonnegotiable.

But what about other things I have learned along the way? Were they true when I was taught them and are they still true today?

What happens when we learn something, trust it to be true and then someone comes along and pops our truth bubble? Do we get confused and begin to question what we know?

I do.

I start to wonder when and where did I learn that, and does it still resonate with me as an adult?

I believe it's a good thing to revisit beliefs we have been taught because there are times when we take on another person's ideas and label them true only to discover they no longer feel right.

Let's say you were raised by non-believers, you might believe there is no God. And then you meet someone who shares with you a different suggestion and you begin to research this new idea. You are invited to their church. You feel welcomed like never before. You listen to the message. It feels good. It resonates with you. And you are invited back.

You are then given the opportunity to look back at what you learned in childhood and now are faced with a dilemma. Do you begin to take on a new path of believing, knowing your parents may feel betrayed when they realize you have abandoned what they believe is right?

Which truth are you going to believe? Yours or theirs?

Learning to trust what you know doesn't just come from books but from life experiences as well. You can read something that sounds good but after checking in with your intuition does it still sound right? Have you gone to your friends who you trust and asked them? Have you prayed about it and asked God for His direction?

In our world today where there is instant information, continually bombarding our heads and confusing our minds, it is paramount to make time to be still.

For me, when I see something on TV or hear something on the news I have a choice.

Do I take sides with those I love because that's what's expected of me, or do I do my own research and come to my own conclusions?

I love my parents and as a child I believed much of what I was taught but as I grew older, I began to question what they thought. Did what they say match what they did? Were they solid in their ideas about church or were the messages mixed?

I had to come to terms with the fact that what I believed as truth was on me and no one else. If I had questions, I needed to do the research. I was the one who had to live with my decisions and if what I was doing felt wrong it didn't matter what they thought. Ultimately, I got to choose because I was going to be the one who paid the price and lived the consequences.

Just because my parents were abusive didn't mean I had to be.

Just because others cheat on their taxes doesn't mean I have to.

Just because the world says to hate others doesn't mean I take up that banner and support that.

I am given the honor and responsibility to make my own choices.

With each passing day I make every effort to pause, take a deep breath and check in with God. I remind myself of the truths that are nonnegotiable. I am mindful of what I am listening to and how it affects me mentally and physically. If something doesn't feel in alignment with me then I can take some time to be quiet and check in. I can seek God's counsel and wisdom. I can change my mind. I can let go of the old to make room for the new.

And I can listen to that small voice inside giving me daily directions on what to do next.

One simple reminder, if you are allergic to something and it makes you deathly ill, would you continue to take it because others do?

I hope not.

If something you have believed in is now making your stomach hurt, giving you headaches, or causing you disease inside your body maybe it's time to honor what your body, mind and spirit are telling you and believe what you know.

✎ Workbook time.

FLUID

CHAPTER 5

Dreaming: Can I Really Have What I Want?

One - Where do I begin?

When it comes to dreaming wouldn't you agree it most likely starts with "Where do I begin?"

Here's the definition of DREAM as a noun:

> *a series of thoughts, images, and <u>sensations</u> occurring in a person's mind during sleep.*

> "I had a recurrent dream about falling from great heights"

> *a <u>cherished</u> aspiration, ambition, or ideal.*

> "I fulfilled a childhood dream when I became champion"

As a verb:

> <u>*indulge*</u> *in <u>daydreams</u> or <u>fantasies</u> about something greatly desired.*

> "She had dreamed of a trip to Italy"

Here we are discussing the cherished aspirations we may have held in childhood.

Where do we begin when it's time to resurrect old dreams we have buried along the path of life?

Did we ever even have a dream of what we wanted to accomplish when we grew up? Did we want to be an astronaut, a nurse, a doctor, or an artist? When we shared our dream with our parents, what was their reaction? Did they tell us our dream was a magical or childish way of thinking and there was no money or security in what we wanted? Did they begin to point out in critical detail why what we desired wouldn't make much money and it was more important to be realistic and go to college? Did they forever bring up following in your dad's or mom's footsteps or being a legacy for the family by doing what they deemed as a valuable profession?

The idea that someone we love knows more about what our hearts want than we do is crazy. Even as children, we have an instinct often clearer than our parents. Our truth hasn't yet been clouded by society's input.

Our ability to dream hasn't been interrupted by someone else's disappointment for not achieving their dreams. We have not yet been influenced to expect rejection or failure when we try. Children don't take failure personally. They just get up and keep going.

The parents often think that if my child doesn't look good in the eyes of society, then I must have failed as a parent.

How many times have we heard the story about someone spending years of their lives in school and are now in debt to pursue a career they never wanted? And only after some kind of crisis do they become brave enough to stop in their tracks, reevaluate what's most important to them and change their course of action?

Why does it take so much anguish to live the life we have been born to live?

When I was young, I wanted to be a social worker, go into the peace corps, or be an attorney. I wanted to go on marches in the street to support the poor. I wanted to defend the less fortunate. I was passionate about social justice. But I had a mother who was afraid, so even the mention of doing anything outside HER comfort zone got squashed. She encouraged me to play it safe.

So I married a divorced alcoholic, had three children, and was left behind when he decided to pursue his dreams.

I recently read in "Jesus Calling," you must relinquish your tendency to play it safe.

God cannot use us if we are continually hiding from His will.

Now we beg the question, "Where do we begin?"

We go back to our childhoods and uncover those things we loved to do when we felt safe and loved.

I would encourage you to grab a journal and sit for a while so your soul can percolate. Get quiet in a place where you can hear your heartbeat. Listen for the small voice that will help you remember.

What were those things that brought you joy?

Were they projects that needed your hands? Did you want to paint, draw, color, or sketch?

Did you want to work alongside your dad when he was doing his woodwork in the garage? Did you want to learn to use the saw, drill, and miter?

Maybe you loved books and dreamed of being a teacher.

Or you watched a grandparent struggle with a serious illness, so you wanted to be a doctor and find a cure for cancer.

Whatever it was, where did it go?

When did you leave the dream behind?

Whose voice told you it was not a worthy aspiration and to pick something more practical?

As you take this discovery journey, be as honest with yourself as possible. No need to blame anyone or anything for your dream being left behind. My next question is, "how happy are you now doing what you are doing?"

We know life isn't all about being happy at the cost of another. We know we may need to rethink leaving our marriage just because we aren't happy. It might feel like a good idea, but is it the right one? If we are feeling unfulfilled, whose responsibility is it to find the things that fill up our emotional, physical, and spiritual cups?

Please know that no one is suggesting you stay in an unsafe place or in an abusive relationship. You are the only one who knows what is right for you and those you love.

I am not one who believes that if you made your bed, you have to lie on it.

That is an old belief I choose not to believe. It's normal to make mistakes, change your mind and then make better and healthier decisions on what your next step is. I am only suggesting that you should not be cavalier when deciding your next big change. Be mindful of when you are rationalizing your decisions to fit what you want but not necessarily what God wants.

Learning the art of pausing can make such an impact on your future.

Maybe now is that time to pause, take a breath and check in with God.

✎ It's that time again to jump into your workbook and keep going.

Two - What do I WANT?

How do I even know what I want when I have believed my whole life that wanting was more about being selfish than kind and loving? Good girls think of others needs before they think of their own. Isn't that what being a good Christian is all about?

I am not sure how I interpreted this message from childhood as being true. I can't even recall if the lesson was taught with words or actions. Or if what I heard was misunderstood because I had faulty filters. Whatever the reason, I took this pattern of thinking way into my adulthood until I was so filled with resentment I could hardly breathe.

What I failed to recognize along the way was the "why" behind my giving. Was I being generous to others as a gift of my love or was it because of something else? Was I showing up to others because I wanted to or because I "should?" Good girls show up right?

I was so darn tired of trying to be good that at some point I just wanted to rebel and quit. To let my selfish nature take over and become a taker instead of a giver.

However, I am coming to believe in order to live an emotionally healthy life, we have to be able to receive as well as give.

So here are a few of the ah ha's I have seen as I continue to do the work I am doing.

- It is safer for me to give. It gives me a sense of control. I get to decide who I give to and why. And there is no feeling of vulnerability when I am the giver.
- My giving was more about holding you hostage to the relationship because how could you abandon me when I had given you so much? I have to tie you to me and create a sense of guilt when you needed to move on.
- I gave to you to try to prove I was worthy of your love.
- I poured everything I had into you in hopes of having you reciprocate. When you didn't, I was resentful and then chose to

feel victimized because you weren't as generous as I was in the relationship.

I was amazed at all the reasons behind what I called "kindness." I really didn't believe I had ulterior motives until I paused and took an honest look at who I had become and understanding how I got here. My intentions were always to help others feel happy and yet, after looking at my motives, I can see there was nothing honest or transparent about how I gave.

With each stone uncovered, I get to see how I did life. I can observe where those patterns came from and, rather than embrace the shame for not knowing sooner, I can celebrate knowing it now. You can't force learning. You will know when you know. But it is paramount you keep showing up each day with an open heart and mind to discover what needs to be healed.

I can choose to either believe in the old ways or give myself space to learn new ways. It won't be an overnight deal. It will take time. With each two steps forward there may be one step backwards. And that's normal. No one can rush the process.

As I now step into new practices of behavior, I have been given opportunities to reframe what I learned from my childhood and create a new and healthier adulthood.

I can see the value in knowing what I want. Knowing and asking for my needs and wants to be honored and met is not an act of selfishness but rather an act of courage. It's totally okay to be clear on what you want so you can be clear with others.

When we know what we want, we don't have to manipulate others to get it. We can be more open and transparent in our communication. We can be direct and open to others saying no as well. Not everything we ask for will be given, but I am finding that when I say it out loud it's easier to accept a no. I can honor another's boundaries as I honor my own.

Now.....

What was the question?

What do I want?

After some serious soul searching, I am discovering I am wanting more a state of being than ways of doing.

I want to live in the energy of trust. Trusting God, trusting myself and knowing who in my life deserves my trust.

I want to live a fluid life of ease, balance, and grace.

I want to keep my focus on me and my relationship with God rather than looking at you and passing judgment.

I want to be kinder to myself so I can be kinder to you.

I want to honor my own personal boundaries and say yes when I mean yes and no when I mean no.

I want to live and love with abandon. Proverbs 19:23 "The fear of the Lord leads to life; then one rests content, untouched by trouble."

And I want to be an example of transparency, honesty, and authenticity so others can find their own courage to do the same.

I want to create a movement where women can find their voices, be brave, change the world for good by standing up and sharing their stories.

 Workbook and journal time. Dig deep. It's worth it.

Three - How do I give myself permission to dream again?

That sounds like an easy question don't you think? But I find many women I have spoken with have a challenge allowing themselves the space and time to just begin.

Maybe it's the way we were raised, or the expectations society has put on us that screams we are not allowed to be that selfish. If we were good women, we would put the needs of others first. We would think of our spouse, children, aging parents before we think of ourselves. But seriously, if that were the case there would never be time for us as those we love would always be needing our time and attention for something.

Is it possible to be good while putting my needs first?

I believe so, but maybe we need to start with addressing the messages passed down for our ancestral women.

On a conversation with a fellow coach a few months ago she spoke of her tendencies to be a perfectionist and a controller. As she shared, I couldn't help but think this wasn't her voice speaking. Who was coming through her telling her she was this way?

I asked her who was speaking through her? She seemed bewildered for a few moments when I asked the question. I went on. I told her I was thinking this might be more about survival skills she had learned along the way, and could they possibly belong to past generations of women who were just simply passing the lessons down to her?

Along with another coach on our call we began to collectively explore what this all could be about. It was really a hunch I had, and I wanted to dig a little deeper.

Here's a little bit of her story on how we came to learn generational lessons being passed down from our ancestors.

Deb Day's maternal great grandmother, Miri, (short for Miriam) was a seamstress who was quite gifted not only with sewing but with keeping things in order.

She believed everything had a place, everything in its place and shared this sentiment with her children.

As I continued to read her story what caught my attention and intrigued me most was the story about her paternal great grandmother, Minna.

Minna, while pregnant, moved from West Prussia, with her family where they lived as farmers to work in industry near the outskirts of Berlin.

Shortly after, her husband was drafted into World War II and later died in France near the end of the war.

Left alone to grieve her loss and raise her small family she continued to put one foot in front of the other just to survive.

She later contracted tuberculosis and died at the age of 42 leaving her daughters Hurta and Helene orphaned at 13 and 14 with other siblings to care for.

The loss was unimaginable for these children and after giving it everything they had, the underage siblings ended up in foster care. It was one more broken heart for this family to endure.

As she shared this little bit of history it became quite clear why Deb carried with her traits of perfectionism and control.

Her female ancestors suffered great loss at such young ages and it would make sense that in order for them to survive their day to day life everything needed to be in perfect order so as not to be blindsided by the unexpected.

As we talked the realization came that much of what Deb lived today was really skills that had been passed down from generations past and she no longer had to embrace those as hers but rather let them go and replace them with new skills.

We can see they may not necessarily be serving us today and those survival techniques were simply taught without anyone being mindful of where they came from or why.

The next step after making these discoveries was to write a letter to her great grandmother, grandmother, and mother in one letter to thank them for all they had handed down and for the incredible skills they had learned along the way to simply survive what they had gone through. I wanted the letter to be a love letter of gratitude but also a letter where she could let them know she was strong enough to let go of what may have helped them but was now only getting in her way of living a more emotionally healthy life.

She could recognize the value of these lessons but break the chain of perfectionism and control by designing her own life using new skills she wanted to replace the outdated ones with.

As we continued with our conversation, we spoke about the value of burning the letter in a special burning pot she could buy which spoke to her when she saw it.

This wasn't going to be a quick process and there was value in taking her time in finding the right piece to use as her sacred pot.

The idea about burning the letter is to release the memories through an action rather than just thinking of what you might say and then letting it go. There is something to actively participating in letting go. The writing it down with pen and paper rather than using a computer. The message travels from your head through your heart and out your hand.

Then there was one more step. It's like when someone you love is cremated and you keep a bit of the ashes to remember who you loved and who you are letting go of. I suggested after she burned the letter and the ashes had cooled down she take a thumb print of the ashes and place the print on a small piece of white paper that she could then place in a small frame as a remembrance of the activity.

I actually went through this process by myself to see how it felt and if I thought it was effective. I took two thumb prints and made it in the shape of a heart and then outlined it in red marker and framed it in a beautiful sea green frame with red matting and have it sitting on my desk.

In those moments when I feel caught in old ways, I can look at the print and remind myself of what I am grateful for and what I am choosing to let go of.

I even did this exercise at a women's retreat in Oregon at a VRBO on the ocean and we stood in a circle with the pot in the middle of the outdoor fire pit listening to the crashing of ocean waves. We each shared a bit about the letter and then, one at a time, we burned our love letters. We had them all together to represent collective healing of all women and went into the house and had each one create their own framed print to take home with them.

Here are a few stories of the women in attendance and how they experienced this exercise.

From Patty Solares-

Of all the activities I have experienced through Susan's coaching, burning the letter of forgiveness to my mom was the most cleansing one.

For a moment, as I was writing it, I felt the resentment, anger and bitterness melt away into the ink of my pen. Then burning it was cathartic.

Placing my thumbs onto the ashes and then forever engraving it onto a piece of paper felt amazing.

Decorating said paper and then putting it into a pretty frame was the ultimate masterpiece.

As I see it on my desk, it's a daily reminder that I gave myself permission to heal, to let go!

I now see my mom with compassion. She did the best she could. She's human.

She made mistakes but so have I. I now allow myself to just feel love. When old thought patterns want to come back, I need only look at my frame….

From Lucia Holman

During our retreat we had the opportunity to write a letter to someone that would then be burned in a release ritual. This letter could be to any one individual, concept, or yourself.

I chose to write to my Mother who passed when I was 22 and she was only 60.

What started out as a letter asking her for forgiveness for the way I treated her out of my selfishness as a teen and young adult turned out to be a love letter to my Mother.

What I had perceived as weakness watching her deal with my narcissistic, rageaholic father was actually incredible strength and her way of protecting me. What I perceived as simple was actually quiet strength of faith and character.

As I wrote out this letter I realized more and more what an incredibly strong woman my Mother had been and how her ways actually built the way for me to be a strong woman and mother to a strong woman and daughter. Because of her my sisters and I and our daughters are strong in mind and spirit. Her selflessness showed me how to be a better citizen of the world.

What started out as an apology turned into a song of praise for a woman who is eternal in my heart and mind. The simple exercise of putting word to paper unleashed such emotions that it resonated for days. Like a deep cleanse as the ash built up from my burning letter my body felt the warmth of joy, the pain of difficult truths, the sweet release of tears mixed with sadness and laughter, and ultimately the peace that resulted of knowing how blessed I am to be my Mother's daughter.

If over the years we have been influenced by the strong women who have gone before us who were taught that having wants, needs and dreams was selfish then those beliefs will be handed down from generation to generation.

We will carry with us ideas that no longer are true for us. Even if they were true many years ago, we don't have to engage with them today.

I don't drive a horse drawn carriage just because my ancestors didn't have a car. Long held beliefs can change as time changes. It's okay to step back, pause and look at where we have come from and what fits with us today. And it's also okay to put down the long list of ideas my parents brought with them from childhood and give those back.

As I travel this journey of self-discovery it becomes evident the value that comes from being brave enough to go looking. It is not an easy task to be willing to face our character defects and ask God to remove them. After all, those habits have served us for a long time.

Old habits have kept us safe and in denial and now the idea of being exposed to others can cause some panic as we grasp to hold on.

But as we continue, we begin to come out of the emotional fog we have been hiding in. We can see the power of God's love as He seeks to heal our hearts and repair our brokenness.

All He asks is that we be open and amenable.

The curious thing about being willing and ready to have God take these defects of character away is there are times when He chooses not to. Just because I am now willing to surrender them doesn't mean He promises to remove them. There are times when He allows them to stay put so He can use them to bring glory out of our state of pain.

Today as I allow myself the space to embrace my healing and forgo living in victimhood, I find it becomes easier to give myself permission to not only dream again but to experience the gifts God has wanted to bless me with all along.

✎ Time to bring out your workbook and open it up to the next set of questions.

Four - Am I willing to allow myself the time and space to start creating my own wish list?

Do you feel it's necessary to include others in your wish list? Or can this just be your own wish list?

I am willing, but actually setting the time commitment to develop my own personal wish list seems to be a different story for me.

The challenge is, or in the past has been to set the time in my calendar and follow through.

Typically I have been a good starter and not too good at finishing.

I come out of the starting gate with tremendous energy and focus and somewhere along the way I see a squirrel and am off and running in a whole new direction.

It could be my tendencies to experience ADD. No diagnosis was made but certainly others observed many of my hyperactive behaviors.

I don't know about you, but I get bored easily and before I can get one task completed I'm off to another one.

Thus my life is scattered all over the place due to unfinished business.

So when asked the question of my willingness to begin my own wish list, the answer is a resounding yes. However, the behavior that follows would indicate more of a no.

Here lies the awareness that something needs to change.

First thing is the permission to break up tasks in a more doable time frame.

There is no way I can sit for 60 minutes and do just one thing.

I need to allow myself maybe 30 minutes, with a five minute break to stand up, grab a glass of water, and just wiggle a little.

Then sit down again and tackle what's left of the remaining activity.

Putting time frames on creative spirits is like trying to drag a cat into a bubble bath so the cat can relax!

Our mode of operation is different.

Our time limits need to be shorter so we can feel like we are making headway and actually accomplishing something rather than feeding our frustration and throwing out the baby with the bath water.

Could my resistance to taking the time to sit and write out the list be only a physical challenge or could there be an underlying feeling of unworthiness and therefore I forgo the activity altogether?

Do I deserve to have a wish list that addresses only my heart's desires? Isn't it being selfish if I don't make sure your wishes are granted first?

Can I still be a kind and loving mother, wife and friend if my bucket list doesn't include those I love?

Am I really allowed to dream on my own?

The answer is absolutely YES!

Who told us we weren't allowed to have our own dreams?

Was it our mothers or grandmothers who were taught that joy was in the sacrifice and that the only way to be truly happy was to give up our desires for the desires of others?

I can only speak for myself, but when my giving becomes lathed with resentment, there is nothing beautiful about how I give.

There is no joy.

Only anger and frustration.

Does that mean I stop giving?

No. It simply means I get to uncover the balance and harmony in my generosity.

I love to give, but not at the expense of my emptiness.

If I can't allow myself permission to dream my own dreams, how can my cup possibly be filled enough to give with a generous heart?

It can't.

And we end up living from a place of scarcity and anger.

We get tired of sharing who we are with the world.

Our spirit starts to dry up.

We lose our voices.

We dim our lights.

And we slowly die while living an unfulfilled life.

That is not how God has called us to live.

There is joy in the morning.

There is hope for a future.

There is love to be shared and communities to be created.

But from a place of fullness and not an empty barrel.

Fill up your cups.

Start with……

1. Use your imagination and if there is somewhere you'd like to explore before your life ends, write it down. If there is more than one place, write them all down. Go to AAA and get brochures of the places you will go. Create a visual collage of the adventures you'd like to take.

2. What is something you'd like to learn before it's too late? Another language? Watercolor painting? Pottery? Cooking dishes from other countries? Check out the summer and fall class schedule of the local colleges. See what they have to offer. If you're a senior, look at the local senior center and see what's available.

3. What's your intuition suggesting you try? A book club with other women. Maybe starting a new Bible study? A hiking club or a

gym membership? You have the answers inside.

4. Have you wondered what it would be like to create your own flower arrangements or if you could make a cherrywood cabinet for your office?

5. Be willing to become your own advocate. Explore possibilities. You don't have to do everything you write down, but please be open to a life where you give yourself the freedom to write your next chapter. The value of being awake and present in the moment as you design this next chapter is that YOU get to be in it as well. It won't just be a segment of caring for family. Carpools and band practices. Ballet and baseball. Back and forth with the kid's crazy schedules. You will be able to write yourself into your story. And as you do, you will find more daily joy to fill up your soul to give to those you love without an agenda.

✎ In your workbook try to be as specific and detailed with your answers as possible.

Five - When I think of my personal wants, what comes up for me?

When I have contemplated what my wants are and if I was willing to receive them, I have hesitated because I was so caught up in what others would think of me if I said yes.

Would I be willing to be brave and speak the truth if I was labeled as hurtful?

Would I be willing to say no if I was labeled as harsh and uncaring?

Would I be willing to be strong and determined if I was l labeled aggressive and ambitious?

Would I be willing to ask for what I want if I would be labeled as selfish?

I'd like to think the answer would be yes today but for a long time I would have hidden behind my face of fear in preparation for rejection.

How long have I lived an unauthentic life trying to figure out what others would think of me if I really was who I was born to be?

Why have I spent years giving my allegiance to other flawed human beings instead of keeping my eyes on God and following His lead and example?

Oh, the years I have wasted caring about something that never really mattered in the first place.

From the long held whispers of what will the neighbors think, to my own fear of rejection and abandonment if I didn't believe the way others did so I would fit in, I gave myself away.

Over and over again.

Over and over again.

Today I am understanding more than what the neighbors think was my parent's way of trying to keep their reputation intact.

Why would the neighbor care diddly squat about what was going on in our house?

I didn't care what was going on in theirs, but there were secrets in our home and my parents wanted to make sure they didn't escape from inside our closed doors.

So I, as a child, kept the secrets.

But now? Am I still needing to keep secrets?

Am I still responsible to carry those survival practices I had in childhood into my adulthood?

Can I finally be free of what the world thinks of me as long as God and I are good?

Can I trust that what I know is what I know, at least for now?

Am I willing?

Who says my dreams today have to be practical?

Who says my hobbies are not worth investing in because they are just hobbies and won't make you money anyway?

Who says my dreams are not worthy of following?

It's not God who says that.

After all isn't He the one who planted that dream in your heart in the first place?

Since I have spent the majority of my life in people pleasing mode it was not an easy assignment to write down a wish list.

I didn't even know what I liked.

I knew what you liked but had no clue what I wanted.

How was I ever going to find out the answer to my question?

Well, I started by visiting my childhood.

What did I enjoy when I was a kid?

I loved everything to do with being creative.

For example: I would take a milk carton, fill it with ice cubes and then pour hot wax into the carton.

When the ice melted and the wax hardened, I removed the carton from the exterior and had my own custom candle.

Or I would take a big candle, melt wax into a small tin, adhere the candle and then burn crayons until the melted colors dropped down the sides of creating a multicolored candle.

Or when I was first married and pregnant with my son, I made a macrame wall hanging the size of our sliding glass doors and used it as a curtain for the large window.

And there were the times I stepped in to offer my help when there was a need in the neighborhood.

Today I can see a common thread being woven throughout the tapestry of my life that involves being creative with my hands and sharing my heart with those less fortunate.

I always thought I would eventually open a craft store, but that never became a reality.

And I wanted to go into the peace corps. That never happened either.

What did happen is I ended up using my creativity with color after I became a beauty consultant with Mary Kay cosmetics. After two years, I stepped into a leadership position as a sales director where I helped women uncover their forgotten dreams and develop their hidden skills.

As time went on, I began to hear the whispers and recognize I wasn't happy here anymore. I was longing for something else. My dreams were changing. My heart for God was changing. But what did that mean exactly?

I knew I needed to let go of Mary Kay. I had outgrown my time there and it no longer felt comfortable wearing the title of Sales Director. I had a sense God was asking me to release it to Him, but I was afraid to let go of the monthly income.

I had been doing 30% of the monthly production to keep our unit alive and our goals as current as they could be. After much internal dialogue and no longer wanting to keep begging God to let me stay, I surrendered. "Okay God. I'll just stop doing all the extra work, the unit will fail, the company will take it away from me and it will all be good."

To my surprise and horror His response went something like this. "Uh no. That's not the way it's going down. Your team will continue to thrive and make production without you. And I still want you to turn it over to Me."

The 64-dollar question was "Which God are you serving? Me or the money God?"

Ouch!

It wasn't too much later I called the company and offered my resignation.

Easy?

Definitely not.

It was painful. I wasn't just walking away from a business I had grown and grown up in, but I was leaving the people I'd been leading for over 2/3 of my lifetime.

I was a loyalist, but I had to recognize where my true loyalties belonged.

I didn't want them to feel abandoned. But the abandonment issue wasn't theirs. It was mine.

I knew in my belly I had made the right decision, and I think we can all agree that following God's lead is truly our heart's desires. But putting the pedal to the metal is a whole different story.

I was afraid they would forget me. I was afraid they'd be angry. I was afraid they would resent me.

I was afraid.

But staying in a place because I was afraid was not the way I wanted to live anymore. I was being dishonest with myself, and I wasn't being fair

FLUID

to my people. They needed someone who could be devoted to them and although my love for them never changed my loyalty to my position had.

Let's take some time to revisit these questions again and go deeper.

✏️ Workbook time, again.

Six- Dream Journal

As we sit and ponder the life we've had and possibly what life we want to create it starts with possibilities. And a little bit of dreaming.

Think on this:

You are the leading lady in the play of your life.

Is she the strong, bold heroine who owns the stage with her courage or is she the victim trapped in the dungeon by a mean king?

We know all about vision boards, but I'd never heard of a dream journal until I got into coaching.

I thought it might be the same thing only in book form, but I am discovering it is so much more.

It's a spiral notebook you can create and use every day as you go on your journey of self-discovery.

Since transformation or renewal takes time, a dream journal can be your diary of changes. You can use words, photos, colors or fabrics.

You can design dream collages of places you'd like to go.

Or the color scheme of the home you'd like to one day live in.

It's like a vision board you can add to as you continue to become the woman God is calling you to be.

I began my dream book, many years ago and for a while I had lost it.

I had put it away in a place and had forgotten about it. As I started digging deeper into my determination to learn who I really was and find my path to a better version of myself, I came across the book.

It's no coincidence that when I was ready the book appeared.

That's how this process works.

You become willing and what you need along the way just shows up.

FLUID

One morning after finding my journal, I sat quietly in the spare room with my favorite coffee in hand and began to flip through the pages.

Memories came flooding back of the photos I had so carefully pasted on the clean white pages.

I had asked some friends I know and trust to write a letter of the things they saw in me that were good. I had struggled for a long time with a sense of "not good enough" and I reached out and asked for help. The letters they wrote ended up really being love letters and I glued each one carefully into my journal for the days when I was feeling lonely and sad and needed reassurance of my goodness.

There were photos of sunrises and sunsets as reminders of the beauty of endings and new beginnings.

There were written entries on days when I was filled to the brim with happiness and days when my heart was breaking.

Words of comfort, encouragement to grow, faith in tomorrow and hope for the future.

Magazine photos of cruise ships to feed my imagination of the places I had been and the places I had yet to explore.

Homes nestled in the trees with warm amber lights shining through the window panes to nudge my soul to rest and be quiet when life gets too busy and overwhelming.

In my journal I could see a documented journey of where I'd come from and a glimpse of who I was becoming.

I had taken magazines of all kinds and on nights when I wasn't particularly interested in watching tv and too tired to read I would peruse my magazines and simply cut out or tear out words and pictures that resonated with me. Colors, shapes, clothes, furniture, designs. Anything that spoke to my soul.

I set my thinking cap aside and let go of the need to analyze why I was choosing what I was. It didn't matter anyway. I had given my soul full reign in choosing what touched her and I would later go back and look with different eyes.

For now, the exercise was just about putting in my book things that made me feel alive, smile, embrace gratitude and tickle my joy.

The curious thing is that throughout the pages, although the pictures and words may have changed, the message from my soul had been pretty consistent.

Let your soul wander in the slow lane.

Breathe a bit more deeply.

Trust in the design of the path ahead.

Value the relationships more than the stuff.

Seek simplicity.

Quiet the mind chatter.

Listen.

Embrace love.

When you think of a dream journal, what's the first thing that comes to mind?

Is the thought positive or negative? Is it: I can't wait to create my own or I could never find the time to do something like this.

What gets in your way of engaging your curiosity? From exploring your world from the inside out?

What dream might still be living below your consciousness that's trying to come alive?

When did you lose your ability to think beyond the limits?

When did the child in you go into hiding taking your dreams with her?

Do you hear her wanting to come out and play again? To remind you of what you used to love.

FLUID

To sit on the kitchen floor and play jacks?

Hopscotch on the front sidewalk?

Coloring with chalk on the cement driveway?

Will you give yourself the chance to explore, adventure, create and imagine?

Let's start here.

1. Look online or check out your local Staples store for a spiral notebook. I suggest it be at least 8x12 and filled with many empty pages. It doesn't have to be pretty, but it helps. Practical is good but beautiful is better.

2. Indulge in a pen that's nice to hold and easy to write with. It feels good in your hand and the ink flows well. Choose whatever color tickles your fancy. Maybe more than one.

3. Gather magazines including the mail order catalogs, Costco monthly or quarterly magazine, consumer reports. You'd be surprised what you find when you really look inside. You can also take yourself on a private date to a local Barnes and Noble, grab your favorite coffee and sit with a few from the rack in the store that have caught your attention. Peruse through a few and take home a couple whose photos really speak to you.

4. Set aside some time, maybe after dinner is done and the family has settled down. Instead of watching television grab your journal, magazines, pen and glue stick and go to a quiet and peaceful place and start your adventure.

It's time to free yourself from living life on automatic pilot and begin showing up to the life you want.

It's possible and so worth the effort.

Put on your adventure glasses and let's take a journey together.

Just remember we are allowed to change our minds and make new choices.

Today is a new day filled with miracles and blessings.

Keep your eyes and ears open!

✎ Open your workbook to your next series of questions and continue your journey of discovery.

Seven- Finding my voice and asking for what I need and want.

As I have grown, I have come to terms with the idea we all have a story and it's important those stories are told.

It's vital to our emotional and spiritual health to share where we have come from and the life experiences that brought us to this point.

It's how we collectively heal our shame and give others hope to believe in their personal value.

How many times have we believed our own inner judge who had told us over and over that our voice doesn't matter? No one cares.

No one is interested in your opinions, ideas, and beliefs. Besides your story is boring, so who would benefit from you telling it.

That voice doesn't speak the truth. It's simply a voice to create confusion and conflict and to feed the belief that we are not enough.

It is definitely not the voice of God.

We were each commissioned to come to this earth and learn the lessons needed to live our best life.

Somewhere along the path of life we may have gotten lost. Our voices were silenced. Our needs ignored. Our wants labeled unnecessary.

It's time to go back and recover that woman who has gone into hiding.

It's time to remind her she is worthy.

It's time to encourage her to speak up. Be brave. Shine her light once again.

IT IS TIME!

When I was a small child there was little time for me. I always thought it was because something was wrong with me.

I know now, as the oldest of five, that with every new addition to our family time and energy had to be readjusted to make sure my younger siblings got what they needed.

Since I was too young to understand I took my parent's behaviors and gave it a meaning that wasn't accurate.

I must have done something that caused them to turn away from me and my needs and wants had no value. That was how I framed it.

Unfortunately for many years I lived out that truth.

Since I was so afraid of rejection and abandonment, each life choice I made was motivated by that fear.

There was no room to step back and think before I made decisions. They were instinctive.

When I met my first husband, who was in the process of divorcing his first wife, I couldn't turn away from his attention because I was terrified if I didn't stay with him, no one else would ever love me.

So I waited until his divorce was final and married him knowing it wasn't the right decision, but too afraid to walk away.

I became embarrassed of my mistakes and felt my story should be hidden from everyone.

Today I know it was shame that kept my truth buried.

Shame stifled my voice.

And as time went along I began to feel choked. I knew I had something to say, but I couldn't find the words.

I was choking on my own need to speak up. It was an awful feeling and I found myself getting angrier and more resentful with every passing day.

I knew there would come a day when I would explode if I didn't find a way to start openly communicating rather than acting out my frustrations.

I went to therapy and sought counsel. It helped, but the true realizations came when I began to turn over the rocks of my life as I studied the tools of life coaching.

Somehow, I was more able to find the roots of where my story began. I could see with more clarity what belonged to others that I took on as mine. How I carried the shame of my parents. How I believed that what the neighbors thought really mattered. How I can now see that the secrets I was hiding were never mine to hide. How I got so mired into my family drama that I couldn't see what was mine and what wasn't.

And how I continued to live my family's story rather than my own personal story.

Was my story covered in shame or was it my family story that had been hidden?

Our stories carry more shame when they are left in the dark closets of our memories. And as long as they are hidden they can never be exposed to light and be healed.

When I began to let the secrets out I discovered there were so many others who came forward to share the same stories.

For so long I felt like I was the only one. I found out there were so many others traveling the same road.

But no one wanted to open up and risk the criticism from others.

The funny thing is once we all knew each other's dark secrets we gathered together in community to encourage one another to grow and heal and the criticism we so feared never actualized.

I think of all the times in the past I let the opinions of others stop me from opening my mouth, believing I would say something wrong. Actually, there is no right or wrong when it comes to ideas, thoughts and feelings.

I gave such power to those who never used their own court to speak their truth.

I don't know about you, but when I ask for what I need and want and I don't get it, I am so much more peaceful when the answer is no.

Most likely it's because I was open, honest and authentic with what I wanted.

I wasn't trying to manipulate others to get my needs met.

I came to the understanding that maybe the need and want was well deserved, but I was asking the wrong person.

Instead of being angry that they said no, or telling myself what I want doesn't matter, I can now embrace the fact that I deserve to have my needs met, but it's important to ask those who are capable of responding with a more positive answer.

I wouldn't be frustrated with someone in a wheelchair if I asked them to help me take down my Christmas lights. I would know they were not capable of doing what I asked.

And yet I will ask someone who is not capable of meeting my emotional needs to give it one more try and then get angry because they can't give me what I want.

That's a sure set up for failure on both our parts.

We don't need anyone's permission to be more authentic, honest and transparent.

We only need our own.

I have discovered it is much easier to tell my story when I have found the courage to forgive those who may have harmed me during the writing of my story.

Forgiveness doesn't mean I allow them the opportunity to keep hurting me. What it does do is allow me to share my past without blame.

I can be objective without pointing fingers at others.

I speak from a place of empowerment rather than victimhood.

I can tell my story with love.

And it makes for a story covered in grace and compassion.

✎ Time to revisit our workbooks.

Eight - Free to be me in all areas of my life.

What does freedom mean to me?
free·dom
/'frēdom
noun

noun: freedom

> 1. *the power or right to act, speak, or think as one wants without hindrance or restraint.*

"We do have some freedom of choice"

Many of us have been denied the opportunity to experience freedom.

It may have begun when we were children living with abusive and controlling parents.

Maybe it was because we had a mom or dad who was sick and we had to be quiet so as to not disrupt the household.

Or there may have been secrets in our home and we felt it our responsibility to keep those secrets so our voice went into hiding.

Or could it be you married a domineering partner and to keep the peace you shut your mouth.

There are many possibilities that could have muted your voice. I'm not sure it matters if we know exactly why as long as we recognize today, we have a different choice.

The reasons we went silent may still exist.

If my parents were alive they may still care what the neighbors think. But that's doesn't mean I have to.

Or there could be someone frail in your home but you are now an adult and know you have a right to say what is necessary for you even if you make the choice not to.

Or your domineering and controlling spouse may not have changed one iota but you believe in boundaries and are now willing to put them in place so you can live a more peaceful life.

Freedom comes when we feel worthy.

Freedom comes when we set boundaries.

Freedom is knowing we have the right to speak and making the choice to either speak up or stay quiet.

Freedom is our birth right.

It has taken me a lifetime to see how my fear of other's anger shut me down.

I went small.

I told myself it wasn't safe to tell the truth.

And as a child that may have been true but as an adult, I no longer have to own that belief.

Patterns of living are created long before we reach middle age.

There is scientific proof that many of our patterns started before we were born.

Whatever was going on with our mothers has been transferred down to us.

I have a couple examples to share.

As you all know I am the oldest of five.

When my mother was pregnant with me she was living with her family of origin in Canada. My dad was on active-duty in the Navy and he was stationed on an aircraft carrier out at sea.

My mom was now without her husband living with her parents and her siblings and hoping my dad would be home in time for my birth.

Based on stories told by her she was 30 days late with delivering me. She was in labor for 36 hours. It was the day after Christmas, it was snowing, and my dad was drunk.

If it took 36 hours for me to arrive, I think I may have been holding on for dear life not sure I wanted to come out! Maybe there was trouble with the birth. For whatever reason it took so long, I now have a deeper understanding as to why I have struggled with the fear of being trapped.

There was a time when I was around eight years old visiting my grandparents in North Carolina.

I had to go to the bathroom, and when I tried to open the stall door it wouldn't open. I felt trapped and I screamed for help. No one came. I finally got the door to open and felt so much shame when I walked out of the restroom fearing that people were looking at me and thinking I was crazy.

Much of my mother's anxiety about whether my dad would be home on time, and just being without her spouse during her first pregnancy, contributed to her own personal angst and mine as well.

I carried her anxiety into my daily life and couldn't figure out where it came from or why. Now I know.

Now let me tell you about my first pregnancy.

My oldest son struggles with anxiety like I do. It has been a lifelong challenge for him.

While I was pregnant with him, I was dealing with his father's abuse of alcohol. My family lived 1500 miles away. I had virtually no support system. I was young, lonely and scared.

I was constantly fearful of whether my husband would come home at night.

Would he be drunk while driving?

Would he die in an accident?

Would I be equipped to handle life without him?

These feelings fed the physical reaction of flight or fight pushing adrenaline into my system which were transferred to my son while in utero. He didn't stand a chance to be emotionally healthy at the time of his birth.

And on top of that, after I got out of recovery the morning of his birth, when I asked for my husband the nurses told me he wasn't there.

When I asked to see my mom they said she was gone too.

He had dropped her back at the apartment so he could go to work.

The first time I held my first born all I could feel was sadness and abandonment.

These feelings are transferred and so we arrive into this world with a sense deep inside that we are not enough or we'll be abandoned, or that the world is not safe.

And we begin to live out those deeply hidden beliefs before we can walk or talk.

We become hyper vigilant. We stand in the corner and observe our environments. We feed the fear that all is not ok.

And we often are not aware we are even doing it.

It becomes our "go to" mode of operation. We go through life unconsciously. We live in an emotional coma.

Until one day an outside circumstance breaks our denial, and we are standing in a storm completely clueless to how we got there.

I lived in what was comfortable for me. I knew what it was like to live in chaos and uncertainty.

In fact, I created situations that replicated my childhood. But I would never acknowledge it.

When I heard a coach say we are winning at the game we're playing I was furious and quite indignant.

How dare you suggest that I am doing this to myself!

I swore I would never marry an alcoholic. There was no way I would repeat what I had endured in my childhood.

Until I married my first alcoholic.

The patterns of behavior were already in place and the roller coaster of my life continued. Therapy helped me get through the first divorce.

Then on to a drug addict.

And more chaos.

Second divorce. More therapy.

Married again. Not an alcoholic or addict but the adult child of an addict mother and 20 years my senior. More therapy.

And then the seeds of coaching began to be planted in my heart, much to my resistance.

First with my female, Christian therapist who asked me if I ever thought about being a life coach.

"Heck no" was my response. "I am a diehard Mary Kay Sales Director and I'm building an empire."

Second seed came when I was visiting my brother in Palo Alto who was staying with my other brother while recuperating from cancer surgery.

I was sharing a glass of wine on the back patio when my sister-in-law asked if I ever considered being a therapist.

I told her the same answer.

But now I was curious.

Was God trying to tell me something? After all, two people had now asked the same question.

Slipping the idea to the back burner of my mind I went on with my life, but the thought nagged at me.

A few months later I looked up becoming a therapist at CBU in Riverside, and a couple online colleges.

$44,000+ and more years of school than I could imagine investing so I let the whole preposterous notion go.

Until I couldn't.

And then lo and behold up came an advertisement for HCI. Health Coach Institute.

It was an online course which could be completed within six months, but each student could take up to a year if needed to become a certified life and health coach. Now the intrigue grabbed hold of me full force.

Could this really be what God was calling me to do in the next chapter of my life?

Seriously I couldn't imagine doing anything other than Mary Kay.

But when the message seemed to be popping up continuously, it was hard to ignore.

And He was so gracious with me. During my many prayers, God reminded me He wasn't asking me to choose. I didn't have to abandon one for the other. I could do both, at least for now. I was extremely relieved.

I scheduled a clarity call with one of their coaches to get more information.

I was hesitant because I was having a difficult time in my marriage and wasn't sure how the next year would play out.

I couldn't conceive training to be a life coach when I was judging my life to be somewhat of a train derailment.

After all, I had three kids with addiction challenges, was on my third marriage and now here I was again trying to figure out what a healthy relationship even looked like.

"God? Really? You must be joking. Who in their right mind would want to be coached by me?"

I kept the appointment and had an insightful conversation. The woman shared she thought I had a lot of wisdom I had garnered through my life challenges and believed I had a lot to offer.

She told me the financial parameters. I said I'd need to give this thought and pray about it. It was quite a financial and time investment and I wanted to be clear this is what I was supposed to do.

I talked it over with my husband and he said "go for it." It's what you were born to do. Just put it on the credit card.

I still resisted. It was the money thing I had struggled with my whole life. If you needed the money for a dream you wanted, I'd work my fanny off to ensure you had what you needed.

But to give myself permission to invest in me? Not as quick to say yes.

In my prayers I came to the understanding if this wasn't what I should do God would be pretty clear. But up to this point His messages seemed to be pointing me to move forward with this training.

The curious thing is how quickly He confirmed my choice.

I called the coach back a few days later and told her "I was all in."

She was thrilled but told me to wait until the following week to register because the company was going to offer a $1500 discount. WHAT????????

I waited. It was Wednesday when I reached her. Again, she told me to wait one more day because the next day it would be another $500 off.

Holy moly!!!!! Seriously!

And then I told my friend Julie, who was also a Mary Kay Sales Director, what I was doing, and she said she wanted to be a coach too and could she join as well.

Sure. I think it would be amazing if we went through this training together.

I called my clarity coach to tell her what Julie was asking and she said if Julie joined, I would get another $500 as a referral bonus.

Could God be any clearer?

In our conversation the following morning He said, "Ok. You get it? I have given you $2500 towards this training. You're not getting any more.

Now it's YOUR turn to step in and do what I'm asking!"

He had been so patient with me, but I think His patience was wearing thin.

I signed up with the intention of keeping my position with Mary Kay and enhancing that business with what I would be learning in this new experience.

It didn't take long for the enemy to boldly show his face.

Two weeks later Joe got a call his best friend of 73 years (from kindergarten) was dying and if he wanted say his goodbyes, we needed to get on a plane and get to Massachusetts quickly.

That was Friday.

We arrived on Monday.

Joe held his hand Tuesday afternoon and ten hours later Bob was gone. And on the same day Bob died, we got a call our dear friend, Robert, back home in California that he had just died a few hours earlier.

We were overwhelmed with sadness. We stayed for Bob's service, cried with his family and headed home for the next celebration of life.

This was the month of August.

In September, my mother died unexpectedly.

I left for Washington the day after the call from my daughter who was in Washington to help care for her.

I carried her ashes home a week later to make arrangements for the burial next to my dad's at the national cemetery.

It wasn't until the week before Thanksgiving that we could all gather to celebrate her life.

In October, Joe got pneumonia and barely made it through without being hospitalized.

In early December Joe any I took our annual trip to Newport, Rhode Island where we stayed at a time share with his other best friend, Dick.

This one was from grammar school that he has known for about 70 years.

While we were there Joe began having incidents of falling.

He leg gave out while he was in the bathroom and again when he was trying to get out of the van that brought us to the airport to return home.

We ended up in the ER a week later only to be told he had Afib and needed a heart procedure.

Do you really want me to go on?

Surgery was successful.

January brought an appointment with a neurologist to let us know Joe had a dropped foot due to back issues and would need a walker.

We hoped it would be temporary.

We were wrong.

I felt inundated with circumstances so far beyond my ability to handle.

But I was determined to not give up on my training.

I managed to squeeze in time to do my studies, follow through with my practice labs and get the homework completed.

I graduated in early April and then took another nine month course to be certified as a mastery and transitional coach as well.

Joe was losing his eyesight due to macular degeneration, gave up his driver's license and now I was learning to be his caregiver.

I had continued to serve my Mary Kay team as their leader while slowly building my practice as a coach.

I could never abandon the people I loved, trained, and supported all these years. However, my heart was being pulled away and I soon realized I didn't have enough in me to give them what they deserved, to follow God's lead into coaching and care for my husband.

The months continued to slowly tick by as the whispers refused to desist.

As witnessed in the chapters prior you all know the struggle I had in letting go.

I knew in my gut it was time to surrender.

But I just wasn't just leaving behind a career I grew up in and given 2/3 of my lifetime too, but I was giving up everything I've known how to do and the confidence I had to do it.

God was gracious and kind. He knew I wasn't ready and he waited until I was.

So after a year of back and forth I was comfortable and feeling peaceful about releasing it. I called the company and told them I was resigning as a sales Director on April 1, 2022, the 41st anniversary of my taking the role at the age of 26.

It was a good decision but definitely not an easy choice.

Along the way, I learned I can't think myself into right behavior. I must behave myself into right thinking.

To become who I was being called to be meant I had to quit dreaming about it and start acting on it.

I couldn't wait to be sure it was the absolute right next step. I had to take the step to build trust I was heading in the right direction.

I couldn't get motivated first to do what I knew was necessary. I had to do what was necessary to get motivated.

When I chose to stop believing my own excuses, put my brave face in front of my scared face and take action, everything changed.

My attitude, my business, my relationships and my ability to love more deeply.

As I write this It has been two years since I retired.

I miss the people.

I grieve the changes in some of the relationships and the loss of others.

FLUID

I embrace the transformation even in the pain.

I stand here knowing I am where I am supposed to be.

It is my desire to help women learn to be quiet, hear the voice of the Holy Spirit, find their voices, speak their truth and write the next chapter of their lives with clarity and joy.

I have never been happier or more peaceful.

Together we grow.

And as we grow we change.

And as we change the world changes.

Here's to our collective courage!

Believe.

I believe.

He believes.

We all believe.

IN YOU!

EPILOGUE:

Living a more fluid life means we make a mindful choice of letting go of the need to live in the past.

We decide where we came from is not where we want to live.

We are willing to do the emotional and spiritual work to be free of old behaviors and thought patterns that keep us in toxic cycles.

We acknowledge we want more out of life.

Not more stuff but more peace.

Inner peace and peace in our relationships.

It can be scary to turn over the rocks in our lives for fear of what we might find.

It's difficult to embrace feelings we have pushed down or hidden over the years.

But those memories and feelings never go away.

They just hide in the shadows of our souls until they are too big to carry and then we get ambushed.

What I am asking you to do is be brave.

Find those long-lost feelings.

Talk about your shame.

Expose your secrets.

Allow yourself space and time to heal.

For it is in finding your authentic voice and the courage to speak it that you will discover what it truly means to be.

It won't be about what you do or who you do it for.

It will simply be about who you BE.

And when you can fully envelop that woman whole heartedly, without judgment, you will find your joy.

P.S. If you find yourself falling behind, please don't give up on yourself or this journey. Remember it's never too late to pick up where you left off and begin again.

Everything that happens is all in God's perfect timing.

Trust that!!!!

To learn more about the author, Susan contact her here: sgoodsonmk@gmail.com

SUSAN E. GOODSON

FLUID

www.ingramcontent.com/pod-product-compliance
Lightning Source LLC
Chambersburg PA
CBHW070100080526
44586CB00013B/1132